Springer Series on Social Work
Albert R. Roberts, D.S.W., Series Editor
Graduate School of Social Work, Rutgers, The State University of New Jersey

Advisory Board: Joseph D. Anderson, D.S.W., Barbara Berkman, D.S.W.,
Paul H. Ephross, Ph.D., Sheldon R. Gelman, Ph.D.
Paul H. Glasser, Ph.D., and Julia Watkins, Ph.D.

Catherine Alter, Ph.D., is Director of the University of Iowa School of Social Work. Her background is in urban and regional planning and social service administration. She teaches research and administration and is interested in the application of microcomputers in social work education.

Wayne Evens is a doctoral student at the University of Iowa. He has a B.A. in behavioral social psychology from Indiana University and an M.S.W. from the University of Iowa School of Social Work. He has experience as a therapist, community psychologist, and mental health administrator. His major interest is the integration of social work research and practice.

Evaluating Your Practice

A Guide to Self-Assessment

Catherine Alter
Wayne Evens

Springer Publishing Company
New York

Springer Publishing Company, Inc.
536 Broadway
New York, NY 10012

90 91 92 93 94 / 5 4 3 2 1

Library of Congress Cataloging-in-Publication Data

Alter, Catherine.
    Evaluating your practice : a guide to self-assessement / Catherine Alter, Wayne Evens.
      p.   cm.—(Springer series on social work ; v. 18)
    Includes bibliographical references.
    ISBN 0-8261-6960-0
    1. Social workers—United States—Self-rating of.   2. Social service—United States—Evaluation. I. Evens, Wayne. II. Title.
III. Series.
    [DNLM: 1. Educational Measurement.   2. Social Work.
W1 SP685SFB
  v. 18 / HV 40 A466e]
  HV40.8.U6A44 1990
  361.3'2'0683—dc20
  DNLM/DLC
for Library of Congress   90-9467
                                                 CIP

Printed in the United States of America

Of the reality or unreality of the mystic's world I know nothing. I have no wish to deny it, nor even to declare that the insight which reveals it is not a genuine insight. What I do wish to maintain—and it is here that the scientific attitude becomes imperative—is that insight, untested and unsupported, is an insufficient guarantee of truth, in spite of the fact that much of the most important truth is suggested by its means.

Bertrand Russel, Mysticism and Logic (p. 16)

Contents

List of Figures and Tables

Introduction

Our goal in writing this book is to make self-assessment accessible to all social workers. There are many reasons why social workers should learn self-assessment skills. Today's need for accountability to clients, organizations, and communities requires that we be able to evaluate our practice; the push for legitimacy and full professional status requires that social work services be effective; and competition for scarce resources requires that social work services be efficient.

Accountability and evaluation of practice sound reasonable, but many practitioners ask, "Accountable to whom and to what end?" They worry that the social worker's goal in doing self-assessment—the improvement of practice skills—may be distorted and the results used for purposes for which they were not intended. Others argue that social work cannot be evaluated, or that it is very difficult to do so.

These concerns are legitimate. There is little doubt that our knowledge about cause and effect in social work is at a rudimentary level. The social and individual problems that social workers face often cannot be easily defined, and even when the problems are clear, the goals for change and the intervention strategies often lack clarity or completeness of specification. And even when these elements can be specified and measured, it is too often the case that the types of problems we must address are often the ones that are the most difficult to change.

This guide was written to lessen some of these fears and address some of these issues and problems. We want to accomplish three major objectives. First, it is our purpose to make self-assessment accessible to all social workers, especially students just starting graduate education and practitioners who have been out of school for many years. We have selected evaluation designs and methods that every social worker can use, regardless of level of expertise. We have tried very hard to write clearly, present directions simply, and illustrate them with many examples representing the breadth of social work practice. It is impossible, however, to describe technologies without using technical terms (some call it "jargon"), but we have tried to define terms carefully and use them consistently. The concern here is not with the technology per se, but with its use in the service of self-assessment. The emphasis is on *doing*.

Our second purpose in writing this book is to include all social workers under the mandate of accountability. There are very fine textbooks available on self-assessment techniques, but they concern themselves almost exclusively with the needs of clinical social work. The goal here is to enlarge the concept of self-assessment to include macro practice as well as micro practice. These methods are suitable for those working in clinical settings as well as in organizations and communities. To demonstrate this point we include synopses of self-assessments done by case managers, supervisors, program planners, administrators, and community organizers and developers.

The most important reason, however, for undertaking this guide is that it gives us the opportunity to clarify what constitutes self-assessment research. There has been much confusion about this subject. *Self-assessment research* has usually been defined as "single-subject research" or, more broadly, "single-system" research. In one sense we believe this is an accurate description; in another sense we believe it is misleading.

It is accurate to say that self-assessment research studies a single individual or group of individuals. We define self-assessment research as research that requires practitioners to examine themselves or their impact on a client/client system. Self-assessment research is unique among research efforts because it has a very narrow purpose; it studies the work of only one person—the researcher—rather than the effect of a program. We point out frequently that the principal feature of self-assessment is that there can be only two things under the microscope—the skill of the social worker or his/ her impact on a client/client system. It is true that "client system" could well mean more than one individual—family, staff, organization, or even an entire community. But the focus of self-assessment research is the skill and effectiveness of you, the social worker.

It is not accurate, however, to say that self-assessment design is single-subject design, if "single-subject" is limited to quasi-experimental time series designs. We believe that self-assessment may be carried out using a multitude of designs available to the social work researcher. It is true that time series designs are the best means of measuring change in individual clients, and we urge their use whenever it is possible and appropriate to do so. There are situations—for example, in group therapy where only pre- and posttests are possible—where a self-assessment design must take on some features of a group design. There is overlap.

The other issue we want to clarify is the question of whether quantitative or qualitative designs are best. We have come to believe that this is a specious argument. Given the nature of social work itself and its maturity as a profession, there is a need for both approaches in the quest for new knowledge. It all depends on the research question. If you are asking the self-assessment question in such a way that you can name, define, and operationalize your concepts (the concepts representing either your intervention or expected client outcomes or both), then you should use a quantitative design. You would be foolish not to, since with quantitative designs data are far more efficiently collected, summarized, and analyzed.

There are many, many situations in social work today, however, when we simply do not know what it is we do. This is not a criticism, it is a simple acknowledgment that the social sciences are immature sciences. We often do not know what it is we do to help clients change; even when we know what we do, we do not understand why what we do brings the change we desire. This is why qualitative designs are so very useful. Qualitative research is the search for definitions and meanings that are the foundation for causal hypotheses.

Campbell and Stanley (1966) have argued that all field evaluations designs are nonexperimental or quasi-experimental because all field research lacks the precise control and randomization that are possible in a laboratory setting. It is beyond the scope of this book to argue what constitutes a "real" experiment; we maintain only that these designs are effective in evaluating practice as it is carried on in social work settings. Many other writers have already provided excellent arguments for the use of these designs in the helping professions.

Because this book is intended as a guide to be used by a diverse range of social workers, it has been organized in a very pragmatic way. After discussing basic issues of self-assessment and its design in Chapter 1, we discuss the research process in Chapter 2. This process then becomes the basis for five self-assessment designs that are described and illustrated for both micro and macro practice in Chapters 3 and 4. Techniques for the analysis of both qualitative and quantitative data are presented in Chapter 5, and issues relating to the validity of self-assessment are discussed in the concluding chapter.

Included in the text are numerous examples drawn from many fields and levels of social work practice. We hope these illustrations will convince the reader that self-assessment need not be a complex and cumbersome process. Indeed, we hope that readers will realize that self-assessment can be a tool for the improvement of practice, rather than an interference with it. This guide is intended as a cookbook of recipes for self-improvement. They have been tested by time and validated by experts.

We would like to acknowledge the contributions of many to the form and substance of this book. Our colleagues at the University of Iowa School of Social Work through many lively debates helped immeasurably as we sought to conceptualize self-assessment as a tool for all social workers. Kristi Nelson, for her enthusiastic support, and John Craft and John Else, for their good questions, deserve special thanks. The manuscript was edited by Beverly Sweet, who can always find time for one more task. And to our spouses, Tom Alter and Sonja Evens, we are indebted for their good ideas, patience, and good humor.

1 Self-Assessment Research

A general description of self-assessment should start by pointing out that the current interest in a scientific approach to social work is certainly not new. Throughout the history of our profession, each new movement or paradigm has attempted to utilize methods that are capable of proof or verification by means of observation or experiment.

The roots of social work are found in the "scientific charity" movement at the turn of the century (Zimbalist, 1983). This movement recognized that the Industrial Revolution had social costs far beyond those that had been anticipated. Its practitioners had an optimistic faith in the capacity of science to remediate the increasing stratification of social class in America and to solve the problems of individuals caught in its dilemmas. They believed the methods of the movement should be those of physical science and that the path to effective answers and outcomes lay in the utilization of rationalized and objective assessment. The images, the language, and the process to be used were those of physical science. Listen to Mary Richmond:

> In the process of our *investigation* of a case, an *inference* may pass through several stages of uncertainty. Its first stage is often tentative. It is a *hypothesis* a possibility to be *proved* or *disproved* by further *evidence*. (Richmond, 1917, p. 83, emphasis added)

The advent of psychoanalytic theory and the various psychosocial schools in the 1920s shifted the focus away from the methods of physical science. Evaluation of practice became primarily a function of supervision, and the focus was on the therapeutic process, not on client outcomes. The research questions were: Is the therapist using her/his technique correctly? What is happening between the practitioner and the client? These methods were qualitative, and the means of assessment relied on the experiences and skills of the supervisor acting as monitor and teacher.

In 1973, the pendulum swung again toward quantitative methods when Joel Fischer asked, "Is Casework Effective?" The ensuing reviews of the available research concluded that there was no evidence that casework did work! The Fischer article put much of the social work profession on the defensive and once again turned attention to outcomes. The issue addressed by Fischer spoke directly to the problems that have plagued not only social work but all of the helping professions—how to demonstrate that what we are doing does what we say it does (Conte & Levy, 1980).

In the 1990s there will continue to be a need for empirical practice, but it will be equally imperative that we both understand the change process itself and be able to predict client outcomes. In order to assist practitioners in these dual directions, many scholars and teachers have suggested single-subject designs and methods (for example, see Bloom, Butch, & Walker, 1979; Gingerich, 1979; Nay, 1979; Neuhring & Pascone, 1986). To these models this guide adds qualitative designs and new ideas about the analysis of data and the application of design to different levels of practice. The most important idea at this point in the development of the social work profession, however, is that it is not an issue of outcome- versus process-focused research. To improve our knowledge and skill requires multiple approaches and a broad repertoire of research skills and techniques.

THE WHY OF SELF-ASSESSMENT

To be truthful, it must be acknowledged that the current interest in an empirical approach to social work outcomes also grew out of the public's disillusionment with "the professions" during the 1960s. Professionals today must justify their decisions, compete for budgets, be explicit about what they do, and prove that what they do has some value. Consumer movements, clients' rights movements, and scarce financial resources all combine to make us all far more concerned with effectiveness and accountability than ever before.

When Fischer (1973) asked, "Is social work effective?" his question was an outgrowth of these events; he raised the accountability issue explicitly for the social work profession and stimulated a lively debate (for example, see Ezell & McNeece, 1986; Rubin, 1985, 1986; Thomas, 1975). As a result, a consensus has developed within the social work profession about the responsibility of practitioners to use the most effective methods available. This trend was codified in 1986 when the Council on Social Work Education adopted a new accreditation standard: all social workers should be able to do self-assessment research.

This ideal is best expressed by Scott Briar (1980a, 1980b). While his model of the accountable social worker is described as the "clinician–scientist," we see no reason why it cannot also describe good macro-level practice as well. We, therefore, prefer the term "practitioner–researcher." According to Briar, social workers must:

1. Use only methods and techniques known to be the most effective.
2. Continuously and rigorously evaluate their own practice.
3. Participate in testing and reporting the effectiveness of their methods.
4. Use untested, unvalidated methods only with adequate controls and only with attention to clients' rights.
5. Communicate the results of testing to others.

We believe, in fact, that most social work practitioners do evaluate their practice. Most are very concerned with the impact they have on their clients, subordinates, organizations, and/or communities. One need only listen to social workers on a coffee break to verify this fact. They ask each other, "What would you do with this client?" "How would you handle this situation?" "How would you intervene in this community problem?" They attend seminars to gain skills and attend case conferences to evaluate treatment plans. Each of these activities is a way of asking, "Am I being effective in my practice?" The problem with these approaches, however, is that they rarely provide feedback that assesses effectiveness of specific interventions with specific clients, nor do they suggest when and where workers need to improve their skills. To be useful, an evaluation system must provide both the agency and the worker with concrete information about what is going well and what is not going so well. It must also provide clear direction for change.

There are good reasons why many social work practitioners are reluctant to formalize their evaluative research. Some believe that what social workers do cannot be evaluated because it is too difficult to measure (Hopps, 1985; Peterson, 1968). Piliavin and McDonald (1978) discuss several reasons why social workers fear evaluation and, therefore, avoid it. They point out the risks involved both in terms of job security and professional pride. Research that fails to demonstrate that casework is effective has not helped this situation; it has, in fact, given social workers good reason to fear research.

We believe, nonetheless, that social workers have a responsibility to evaluate their practice because evaluation enables us to improve our practice and because theories about social problems and change will not be advanced until we are able to aggregate knowledge about what works gained by hundreds and thousands of social workers who invest time and effort in self-study. Indeed, the proper answer to the criticism that casework does not work is to accumulate evidence that it does. A commitment to self-assessment, in our view, is the mark of a professional. In other words, social work practitioners must now become professionals, assured of their practice effectiveness and held accountable for it.

PROFESSIONALISM

Current interest in a scientific approach to social work is a result of the increasing "professionalism" of social work practice. As the youngest of the helping professions, social work is still developing in two important ways. First, the profession is defining its standards. Time and effort are spent in establishing licensing laws, certification, accreditation standards, and eligibility for third-party reimbursement.

Second, there is concern about the moral dimension of professionalism. Reamer (1982) has said that ethics are the soul of a profession and has urged the social work profession to develop its code beyond its current set of canons, which are often not explicit and can, in practice, often be in conflict. He cites the National Association of Social Workers' Code of Ethics, which states, "the social worker should serve clients with devotion, loyalty, determination, and the *maximum application of professional skill and competence*" (NASW, 1980, emphasis added). Reading this, we might ask, but what is "professional" skill and competence?

One way of getting at the meaning of this term is by means of moral philosophy. For example, Bernard Gert (1973) lists 10 rules that he hypothesizes all rational people accept as standards for ethical behavior:

1. Don't kill.
2. Don't cause pain (both physical and mental pain).
3. Don't disable.
4. Don't deprive of freedom or opportunity.
5. Don't deprive of pleasure.
6. Don't deceive.
7. Keep your promise.
8. Don't cheat.
9. Obey the law.
10. Do your duty.

The last, Rule 10, has a unique function for people who voluntarily join a profession. Rule 10 asserts that professional membership raises us to a higher level of responsibility than nonprofessionals because to "do your duty" for a professional requires adherence to the profession's code of conduct in addition to the more general rules of moral behavior embedded in religion, civil laws, custom, and society (summarized by Rules 1 through 9).

When we elect to become social workers, then, we are *morally* bound by the NASW Code of Conduct, which requires us to practice with the "maximum application of professional skill and competence . . . and to continuously improving practice." This is just another way of saying that social workers must engage in self-assessment. The essence of professionalism, the core of the Code to which we are bound, is that our practice shall be self-critical, self-correcting, and self-improving. There are many practice principles embedded in this concept of professional practice; two are particularly relevant here.

Responsibility to Specify the Intervention

Reamer (1982) also points out that social workers face many ethical dilemmas that are not clearly addressed by their Code because there are many situations where two rules apply simultaneously. Consider two of Gert's rules: "don't cause pain" and "don't deceive." There are many cases where to tell the truth will cause the client pain and where deception is necessary in order to achieve a therapeutic outcome. When faced with ethical dilemmas of this kind, professionals must: (1) be sensitive to the fact that they are breaking a moral rule, (2) specify for themselves the intervention, and (3) be able to rationally justify the intervention.

The concept of public advocacy (Gert, 1973) is useful in this context because it is a standard to apply when you contemplate breaking a moral rule. Public advocacy requires that you be able to construct a rational argument in defense of your actions when choosing to violate a moral rule (and be willing to justify yourself openly with family members, other professionals, and administrators). Such an argument should contain several elements. First, you must state the prior conditions that justify deviance from the rule. Second, the violation (and the intervention of which it is a part) must be specified and carried out in a consistent fashion. Third, you must demonstrate that the violation causes no greater harm than obeying the rule would have done. It is important to remember that the justification has to be such that a rational person would understand it, not that a rational person would, of necessity, accept it.

Too often social workers are not prepared to justify their practice choices (Briar, 1980a; Fischer, 1978). We often are hard-pressed to present a convincing case for what we do, especially when confronted with opposing views from other professionals. Too often our justification is, "I know when I'm being effective, it felt right," or "this (not specifying what this is) is consistent with my values." It is questionable whether a rational person would understand any of these arguments.

We are not asserting that social workers should not use their experience, intuition, values, beliefs—that there is anything wrong with having a preferred style of therapy or intervention. We are asserting that, especially in those cases where interventions are going to violate an ethical rule, there must be explicit and rational reasons for such a course of action.

Professionals have an ethical responsibility to state the hypothesis on which their intervention is based whenever possible and to operationally define their actions. This is easily said, of course, but may take years to accomplish. Nelsen states in her conclusion (1985, p. 8):

> By verifying their use of interventions . . . [professionals] . . . strengthen the credibility of their published reports of such projects. They also help readers of the reports to understand much more fully the nuances of the interventions used. This enhances what readers can learn from a project and makes it possible to carry out accurate replications of single subject studies. Careful verification offers . . . [professionals] . . . who are conducting projects an additional benefit. By devising operational definitions and coding their tapes, they become much more aware than they would otherwise have been of what *they actually did* in interviews that turned out to help or not help their clients. This strengthens the practitioners' clinical knowledge and skills. (emphasis added)

Responsibility to Use Only Effective Interventions

Specifying the intervention is only the first ethical responsibility of professional practice. Professionalism also requires that, to the greatest extent possible, only interventions known to be effective will be used. This is only common sense. You would not take your child to someone for orthodontics if you knew he or she had had poor results in straightening teeth. Of course, individuals, organizations, and communities are not teeth.

"Maximum application of professional skill and competence" means that clients know what they are getting, and get what they pay for. This requires that every social work practitioner and human service organization make ethical and philosophical decisions about what their interventions are seeking to achieve and, further, use evaluative research to assure that they are achieving what they say they are. When self-assessment designs are used on a routine and systematic basis, it is possible to determine if practice is doing the things it claims to do and whether these things are effective in achieving the purpose as specified. This is the line between professionalism and quackery.

On the other side of the issue, social workers must always bear in mind the limitations of their particular strategy and the risk of generalizing from small amounts of information. The results of evaluative research are no better than the inputs; that is, the concepts used, the measurement tools, the data collection methods, and so forth. When we employ a research method there is always a tendency to believe that if information is presented in a rational and/or statistical way it somehow becomes nearly infallible. This, too, is a violation of professional ethics and of the scientific attitude that requires multiple demonstrations before a position has any believability.

Social workers, if they are to be professionals, must be willing to approach their claims of effectiveness with skepticism. Indeed, the difference between a theory and an ideology is that a theory is always negatable, whereas an ideology is never even tested. Self-assessment means testing ourselves in a lifelong commitment to theory construction, knowledge-building, and excellence in practice.

THE HOW OF SELF-ASSESSMENT

The best justification for using an intervention is to have personal evidence that it works well with your specific type of client within your client's specific context. You may be convinced of the necessity for self-assessment, yet not at all sure how to uncover this evidence. The question of *how* to do self-assessment is the important one. In approaching this question, we must confront two basic issues: what design approach to use and what research process will be the most useful.

There are two basic approaches to the design of self-assessment research: nomothetic (group designs) and idiographic (single-system design). Each has a different purpose, each provides a different kind of knowledge (Jayaratne, 1978), and each has its own distinct literatures. Both approaches are necessary for the development of social work knowledge.

Group Designs

A general description of group designs starts by pointing out that they require the collection of data at one (or a limited number) point in time from multiple subjects that represent (are samples of) a population of interest. Group designs are used when researchers want to test whether theories can be generalized to large populations, and they therefore necessitate the use of sampling (probability) theory A wide array of data collection instruments can be used with group designs, such as surveys, behavioral measures, and standardized measurement tools, and different analytic methodologies that range from qualitative to highly quantitative are also available.

A Group Design

Family and Children Agency (F & C) is a private not-for-profit organization in a medium-size city in the southwest. It started many years ago as a child welfare agency doing foster care and adoption. In recent years F & C has become a family-based agency with multiple programs, the largest of which is a unit that accepts referrals from the State Department of Human Services (DHS) for treatment of families at risk of out-of-home placement due to child abuse.

The supervisor of the family treatment unit is Miriam Sears. Several years ago she began to think seriously about a staff development program for her unit and realized that in order to help staff improve their skills and effectiveness they had to have a means of identifying the areas where they were inadequate. As a result, Miriam began to help each of her staff assess the effectiveness of their work with their families.

In a series of staff meetings, the design of self-assessment was discussed. Miriam stated that the design must start by specifying clearly the problem that caused the referral from DHS. The staff stated that in most cases the referring problem was parents' inability to manage stress and control anger, the consequence of which was a tendency toward violent striking-out behavior. The goal of their intervention, they concluded, was to enable parents to change their behavior, to learn to manage stress without resorting to physical violence.

Sarah was the first staff member to actually design and implement a self-assessment project with Miriam's help. As families were substantiated for abuse by the intake unit at DHS, they were randomly assigned in two groups: the family unit at DHS and Sarah's caseload at F & C. Each parent was then given a test that had been shown to be a valid measure of proneness to violence (Whiteman, Fanshel, & Grundy, 1987). It used role-playing scripts in which the parent played someone confronted with a very provocative child, followed by a series of questions about feelings, reactions, and behaviors to these situations. When the treatment was completed and the case was being closed, the proneness to violence test was repeated.

It took 2 years for both the DHS unit and Sarah to open, treat, and terminate 30 families. When the study ended, Sarah analyzed the data as follows. For each group she computed the average amount of change in proneness that had occurred between intake and termination. Clearly Sarah's group had changed the most because its average score was 48.7 points lower than the DHS group's average score. She put these data on a graph (see Figure 1.1).

FIGURE 1.1. Comparison between two groups on extent of change in their proneness to anger as a result of treatment.

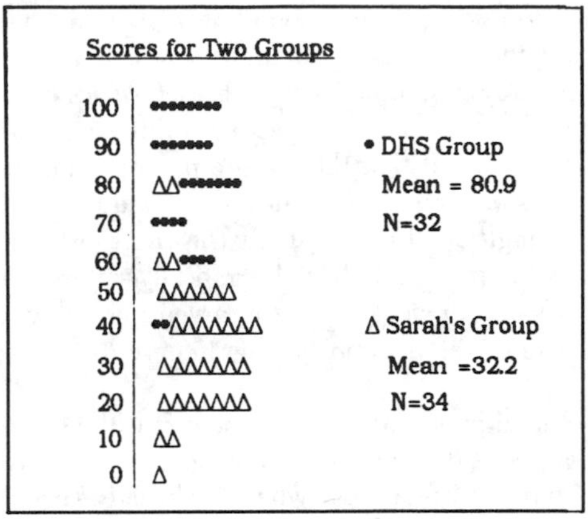

```
            Scores for Two Groups

      100 |  ••••••••
       90 |  •••••••               • DHS Group
       80 |  ΔΔ••••••••              Mean = 80.9
       70 |  ••••                    N=32
       60 |  ΔΔ••••
       50 |  ΔΔΔΔΔΔ
       40 |  ••ΔΔΔΔΔΔ               Δ Sarah's Group
       30 |  ΔΔΔΔΔΔ                   Mean =32.2
       20 |  ΔΔΔΔΔΔ                   N=34
       10 |  ΔΔ
        0 |  Δ
```

On the day Sarah presented her findings at a staff meeting, she proudly reported that the clients referred to her had, on the average, improved more than the clients that had been treated at DHS. Further, she said that by computing a statistic, she knew that there was less than a 5% chance that this difference between the change scores was due only to chance.

There was a troublemaker on the staff, however, and his name was Steve. He looked at the findings and immediately said that if the difference in change scores wasn't due to chance, maybe it was due to something else—and a something that wasn't Sarah's skill. Maybe, he said, there was some factor at work that made Sarah's group more amenable to treatment. Maybe DHS referred only the "best" parents to Sarah, or maybe Sarah's children were less provocative than the DHS children—neither factor having anything to do with Sarah.

Miriam patiently pointed out to Steve that the project was designed to guard against these threats to its validity. First, she said, the families were randomly assigned to Sarah's group and the DHS group so that characteristics associated with the parents or children would be evenly distributed across the groups. Second, she said, Sarah studied *all* her client families. By looking at the coping skills of all her families, she could see that if, on average, her caseload behaved differently (scores lower on the proneness to violence test) than the DHS group, then she could assume that the difference was due to her intervention skill. By randomly assigning families and by studying at least 30 families in each group, said Miriam, it could be assumed that the unmotivated and low-functioning parents were evenly distributed across the two groups. The idea was that there were examples of all sorts of parents in both groups, so the test was fair because, *on the average*, the groups were alike to start with.

But Steve wasn't ready to give up. He acknowledged that on the whole it was clear that Sarah's group had improved the most. But, he said, he couldn't understand how knowing that helped Sarah all that much! Looking at Sarah's graph, he observed that there were four families that scored as high or higher than families in the DHS group. Steve asked Sarah if she had any idea why these particular families were not responding to her intervention. In other words, he said, did the study give her information that would allow her to differentiate her therapy based on specific characteristics of the client family?

Steve said he was particularly interested in this question because he had observed among his caseload that there were parents who responded to him in very different ways. Therapy sometimes weakened the coping skills of parents rather than strengthened them, at least in the short run. Furthermore, he said, sometimes his parents behaved erratically—their behavior changed from day to day or week to week during intervention. How, he asked, could he begin to understand this reaction to his intervention if all the measures were averaged?

Miriam intervened by saying she was sorry, but the group design chosen by Sarah could not get at this question about specific client reactions to therapy. She pointed out, however, that what Sarah had learned was extremely helpful in showing DHS, which funded the F & C unit, that their child abuse treatment program was very effective in achieving the goals of treatment and that the funding should therefore continue.

This scenario about Sarah and her self-assessment at Family and Children Agency describes in a general way the major features of group designs. They require a large number of randomly selected or assigned subjects that are tested/measured on a selected behavior at one/two points in time. Further, the results of group designs are often summarized using statistical procedures.

While group approaches are useful to theoreticians, administrators, planners, and policymakers (those needing generalized information about larger numbers of people), they are of less value to individual practitioners who want to evaluate their efforts during single interventions. When doing nomothetic research, for example, the researcher is not concerned with the behavior of any given subject but wants to know, in general and with other factors being equal, how humans behave in a given situation. Most of the rules of learning, for example, were derived from this type of research. This approach is very effective in both predicting and evaluating on a large scale.

Problems occur, however, when one tries to apply this approach to a unique individual. In using these approaches, the researcher has a small sample of the behavior of interest from a large number of subjects and the results are reported as a probability statement. Results from group designs may lack usefulness to a single practitioner because:

1. Group designs represent one slice in time; they do not illustrate a pattern of behavior or behavioral change.
2. With group designs there is no way of disentangling preexisting individual differences from individual difference in change over time unless experimental conditions exist, which they seldom if ever do in agency and field settings.

For these reasons, many practitioners now advocate the single-system approach as a means of gaining a better understanding of one's differential effect on individual clients.

Single-System Designs

Single-system approaches are an alternative to group designs. The single biggest difference in the two approaches is that single-system designs collect data at multiple points in time from an individual or individual client system. In other words, repeated measures substitute for the multiple subjects. Also known as the clinical approach, these designs allow the practitioner to study one entity (it could be himself/herself or the client/client system) in a concentrated manner over time in order to discover patterns of change. When a large number of single-system designs have been accumulated, then the results can be aggregated to make a summary finding about the effectiveness of the program as a whole.

Like group approaches, single-system designs vary greatly. At the qualitative end of the continuum are nonmanipulative observations of one client/client system known as *case studies*. More quantitative, yet not experimental, are studies that makes multiple observations of a behavior or trait that can be counted or measured as a quantity. At the other end of the continuum are the experimental designs that control the influence of extraneous environmental factors.

A Single-System Design

Steve decided to take another tack for his self-assessment because he wanted to be able to gain information about similarities and differences among his clients as well as learning something about the outcomes of his interventions. He decided to try a single-system design. Steve knew that to get a clear picture of his effect on a client, the timing of the measurement would be crucial. He couldn't rely on just two observations but would have to have many.

His next referral was a single mother named Madelaine who had two preschool children. He used the first month to develop the therapeutic relationship and for diagnostic purposes. When he felt he had established sufficient rapport and trust, he asked Madelaine to estimate the number of times per week in the past that she felt prone to violence (felt she was in danger of exploding and losing control of her behavior). Then Steve asked her to observe her own behavior and to record instances of proneness to violence on a daily basis. Steve recorded Madelaine's self-reported observations by the week on a line chart.

At the end of 4 months Steve presented the findings of his study at a staff meeting. He explained that he had used Madelaine's estimate of her prior behavior to create a baseline during the intake phase. Beginning at week five he relied on her observations, but he had corroborated her self-reports with observations from the day care center. He said he felt these were reliable data.

Miriam commented that the data clearly showed that Steve's intensive in-home work with Madelaine was having the desired effect, but asked if he had clues to the cause of the reverse in the trend during the 10th and 11th weeks. Steve referred to his line chart (see Figure 1.2).

FIGURE 1.2. Line chart of Madelaine's scores on proneness to violence scale across 16 weeks.

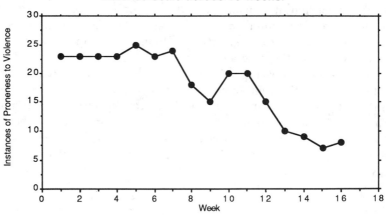

Steve replied that Madelaine's mother had visited from another state and he felt that since Madelaine was planning on moving to her mother's home it was imperative to include her mother in the therapy, or to enable Madelaine to make other living arrangements. This, then, became the focus of the next phase of Steve's intervention plan with Madelaine.

Steve concluded his presentation by saying that he was glad that Madelaine had been the subject of his first single-system design because he felt that his approach to in-home family-based treatment was most effective with isolated single mothers, especially if they were adult victims of abuse. He said his next case would be a two-parent intact family, giving him a chance to look at a different pattern of behavior during treatment.

We believe that client/client system research, if it is to be most useful to the practitioner, is best described by a repeated assessment of the client/client system as change occurs over time. We agree with Kratochwill (1978), who argued that in research on social work practice an idiographic approach is required by the very nature of the enterprise. He held that a practitioner is always working with a specific individual/system in a specific environment; therefore, other things are *never* equal. He concluded that when the target is an individual, evaluation must be idiographic in nature to be effective. Group data may, in fact, be useless for answering the questions that social workers need to ask about themselves and their practice.

Social workers engaged in self-assessment are interested in their effect on specific individuals or systems, not in the probability that change will occur in an individual or population. For example, a group study might show a statistically significant reduction in spouse abuse among an agency's clients. A reduction from five incidents of violence per month to two incidents per month, although statistically significant in a large group, does not satisfy the clinical need for no violence in the family. Another group study may show a statistically significant 10% reduction in poverty in a segment of a city, but the community organizer may say that this is meaningless because there are still 1,000 families living without adequate food and housing in her specific neighborhood. A 20% improvement in lag time in getting case notes recorded may please an administrator, until it becomes clear that two staff members who were doing poorly have improved a great deal while four other staff have begun doing somewhat worse. In short, grouped data may mask a number of important facts that are crucial for a differential understanding of effectiveness.

Single-system designs focus on *specific interactions* between *a specific practitioner* and *a specific client or client system*. The practitioner gathers a large sample of behavior of a single system—the focus is how the system behaves/feels/performs/interacts in a large number of situations. We believe the type of knowledge needed by individual practitioners is best obtained in this way. This is, to be sure, a reductionist approach, and it is not the only approach. It is the best means, however, that practitioners can use to study their own practice effectiveness.

Having espoused the case for an idiographic approach, we must conclude with a caveat. There are social work settings and social work interventions where effective self-assessment designs will appear to be closer to a nomothetic than to idiographic design. Whenever the purpose is to study a practitioner's effect on a collective of individuals—as in group therapy, supervision, or community organizing—then reliable results will depend upon information being collected from multiple sources. Data from multiple respondents do not necessarily mean that the clinical approach has been abandoned. Idiographic design applied to self-assessment requires only two principles—focus on the skill or outcomes of a single practitioner and multiple measures over time. These two objectives, in certain practice settings and in certain social work roles, can only be achieved via multiple sources of data.

DEDUCTIVE REASONING VERSUS INDUCTIVE REASONING

The social work profession needs two things. We need principles, rules, and concepts that can be used to explain, understand, and predict the behavior of clients/client systems. At the same time, practitioners must be able to work differentially with clients having idiosyncratic problems. The former requires convergent and parsimonious knowledge (Jayaratne & Levy, 1979; Siegel, 1984); the latter calls for divergent and expansive knowledge (Glaser & Strauss, 1967; Shontz & Rosenak, 1985). The first reduces concepts to general theoretical statements; the second provides many ways of thinking about clients and their problems.

Convergent Knowledge

Research designs aiming to establish convergent knowledge look for typical patterns of behavior by which people experience their problems. Deductive research proceeds from the assumption that (1) diverse problems can be grouped into a small number of categories that explain behaviors and behavioral patterns, and (2) general principles of intervention can be deduced from this theory that can then be validated against the results of experimental tests.

- If you are doing a deductive study, you begin with an abstract theory about yourself or your client/client system and end by drawing concrete conclusions from your observations. These results will either reinforce your theory or cause you to modify it.

The search for convergent knowledge has occurred much more frequently in clinical settings than in community settings. This need not be so, as illustrated by the following report.

A Deductive Study

Sally, a community organizer, was working for a coalition of organizations concerned with public housing in a midwestern city. The coalition had recently completed a needs assessment of the city's public housing stock and had found that it was deteriorating due to vandalism, misuse by resident families, and inadequate budgets for maintenance. In subsequent discussions it was decided that there was little chance of improving the situation unless all three causes were attacked simultaneously. Sally was assigned the task of improving the ways in which the residents took care of their apartments and the common areas. Sally knew she had the problem and goal already defined for her. She decided to test three intervention strategies that she had been thinking about by using a single-system multiple-baseline design (see Chapter 4 for a description of this design). She chose one complex in which to implement a very directive approach with negative consequences, one complex in which to implement a recreational program for resident children to keep them busy, and one complex where she would establish a tenants' organization by using community organizing principles. Her study required a baseline monitoring period of 2 months at the three complexes while she measured the normal incidence of misuse and destruction of the physical property. She then began the three different interventions and ran them for a period of 6 months, taking measurements of misuse every week. At the end of the intervention period she returned to the baseline condition by withdrawing the programs but continuing to take measures every week for 6 more months. The data showed that, although the amount of property damage had been identical in the complexes during the baseline period, the complex that had developed the tenants' organization had far less misuse during the program period. Further, at withdrawal the complexes with the negative and positive reinforcement returned to the level of property damage they had had during the baseline period, but the complex with the self-help approach experienced carryover effects and did not return to the baseline level. As a result of this study, the coalition sought and received funds to renovate the apartments and to support tenant organizations in all their facilities.

Divergent Knowledge

Research designs aiming to uncover divergent knowledge are built on the premise that individuals experience and express their problems in widely varying ways. They proceed from the assumptions that (1) problems with which social workers must deal are so diverse that no single empirical measurement tool is adequate for capturing the data, and (2) intervention techniques are so numerous that no single set of data collection procedures is adequate.

- If you are doing an inductive study, you start from divergent concrete reality and work toward the abstract. You begin the process by collecting data and finish the study by formulating an abstract theory and deriving a hypothesis from it to be tested by another study.

Because of the structure afforded by clinical settings, some researchers believe that in clinical settings only deductive designs should be done. There are situations, however, where so little is known about the presenting problem that only a qualitative exploratory process is appropriate. The following study is an example in which, even though the practitioner did not have to face difficult control issues associated with field research, there was little experience or theoretical foundation on which to build a deductive design. Jim was prudent to start with an inductive design.

An Inductive Study

Jim, a hospital social worker, was assigned to a floor that had been reserved for AIDS victims. The goal of his intervention was to "improve the quality of life" of these terminally ill patients. Jim felt overwhelmed and therefore decided to begin a research project. His purpose was to better understand his patients' adapting mechanisms so he could enable them to strengthen and develop their capacity to relate to him. Because he could find little in the literature to guide him, and no theoretical perspective had been shown to be useful with this patient population, he decided to do an exploratory inductive study—to study these patients without first defining their problems or choosing measurement tools (see Chapter 2 for a description of this design). Jim studied six patients; he extended the routine initial interview into a full case study. When he analyzed these data, the results suggested—although they did not prove—several useful pieces of information. Foremost was that these patients had very different personalities and, therefore, were trying to cope with their crises in very different ways. It appeared to him that these personality types could perhaps be grouped into two categories, inner-focused and outward-focused, and that these types of persons required different types of responses from him to bring about effective changes in their coping skills. This conclusion of Jim's exploratory study enabled him to begin to differentiate his intervention and was the springboard for his next round of research, when he tested the effects of structured and unstructured interaction on AIDS patients with different personality types.

These two studies illustrate that idiographic research is a large class of designs that focus on an individual person or system as the subject and that vary widely in the degree to which they search for convergent or divergent knowledge. As should be obvious from these illustrations, it is the attributes of the programmatic area you are working with that determine your approach to designing self-assessment projects.

The point is that there is no one right way to do self-assessment. You can complete the research process starting from any point. In fact, accumulating practice knowledge requires both processes. Single-system designs can be deductive and can be used to test concepts and intervention techniques against general practice theories (and thereby further develop the theory). On the other hand, single-system designs can be inductive; they can generate a rich body of descriptive and explanatory knowledge about clients and client systems that have vastly different characteristics, problems, and intervention potentials.

Social work practitioners must understand that different designs serve different purposes, and then choose a design that fulfills their needs at the time. Sometimes we are very experienced in working with a specific problem and are able to test a theory or technique we have been developing. But sometimes we are not, and laying the groundwork by identifying appropriate concepts and patterns of behavior is the most useful approach we can take.

2 Designing Self-Assessments

All types of research follow a similar research process regardless of whether their purpose is to generate basic knowledge or to do self-assessment or program evaluation (Cole, 1976; Wallace, 1971). This process has four steps (see Figure 2.1):

FIGURE 2.1. The research process.

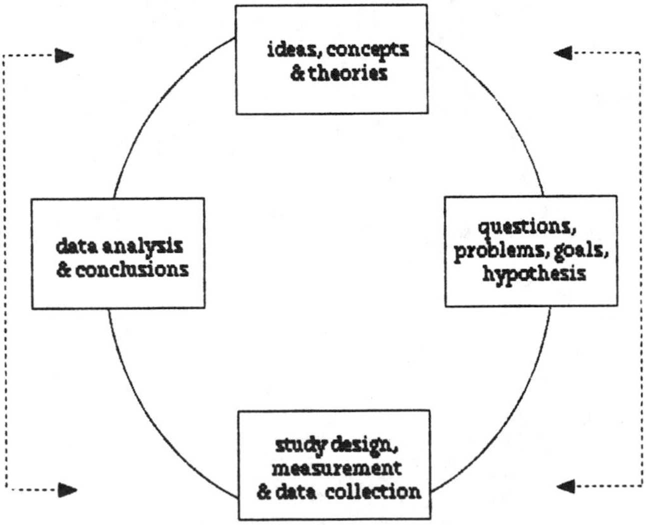

- Formulating ideas, concepts, and practice theories.
- Formulating research questions, problems, goals, and hypotheses.

- Selecting a design and methods for measurement and data collection.
- Analyzing data and drawing conclusions.

Each of these four steps includes a cluster of activities, and each step is usually completed sequentially. These steps are often depicted as a circle because *the research process, when completed, always brings you back to where you started*. However, the steps are sometimes depicted as a spiral because successive iterations of the process return your research to increasingly higher conceptual levels. This is a useful image because it underscores two very important features of the self-assessment. First, the process has no particular beginning or end; the results gained from one cycle become the starting point for the next cycle, and your knowledge base is continuously enlarged. This is not, then, a linear process, but one of successive iterations throughout your professional career.

The second important idea conveyed by the circle is that *the process can be entered at any point*. There has been, and continues to be, a great deal of discussion among practitioner–researchers about the best way to approach evaluative research. The disagreements often boil down to an argument about inductive versus deductive approaches. Because it is necessary to understand this issue in order to use the research process effectively, we discussed it at length in Chapter 1.

Having said that you can enter the circle at any step, and because we must start somewhere, we elect to describe the research process by starting at the top of the circle. Our approach is therefore deductive. This choice is not meant to imply a preference for the deductive, but is only a practical necessity.

If you plan a deductive study, you start with a theory (step 1) and hypothesis (step 2) and collect data (step 3) and analyze them (step 4) in order to confirm or disconfirm the theory. Deduction is the process of logical reasoning from an abstract generalization to a concrete conclusion. To understand deductive reasoning, then, we must start with the formulating of abstract generalizations.

FORMULATING IDEAS, CONCEPTS, AND PRACTICE THEORIES

Formulating Ideas

Our actions and emotions are shaped by our ideas. Ideas are the means by which we organize the chaos of the concrete world that surrounds us. They are images existing in the mind, consciously or unconsciously and actually or potentially, as a product of a mental activity such as a thought or conception.

All social work practitioners have ideas about what interventions work, with whom, and under what conditions. They also have ideas about why these interventions work. Often these ideas and theories are obtained from reading professional journals. Most often they are obtained from practice.

Ideas can be elusive. Many of our actions in practice are driven by intuition gained from experience. Often we have ideas but have never conscientiously clarified them or made them explicit. The cognitive process of building theory from ideas requires time, energy, and persistence and is not an activity that comes easily to many clinicians and administrators (those who are naturally more at home with inductive thought processes).

Regardless of the origin of your ideas, self-assessment in a deductive mode cannot occur without the formulation of theory. This requires you to step back from day-to-day activities and focus on what you are doing. This important step—and often the one that takes the longest—is the refining of your ideas into concepts and combining these concepts into theories that can be tested.

Formulating Ideas

Edna is a program planner who works for the regional planning authority and has had 20 years of experience in developing community-based service systems. To understand the context of her work, she routinely reads a number of academic journals in her field (e.g., *Administration in Social Work*, *Academy of Management Journal*). From research articles and from her own experience, she began years ago to formulate ideas about how organizations work together when pursuing common goals. The unusual thing about Edna is that she has made a deliberate effort over time to state explicitly her working theories for herself and others. Edna has written: "Autonomous human service organizations—both public and private—develop relationships with each other much like divisions and departments in very large organizations. The basis for these relationships is usually the exchange of resources (e.g., clients, physical or intangible assets, information, legitimacy, etc.) or the pursuit of common goals (e.g., to effectively service a common client population, to research and develop a new program, etc.). The degree to which organizations will exchange and cooperate with others is dependent on: (1) their inability to achieve a needed goal on their own, and (2) their perception of the benefits to be gained from cooperation balanced against the costs. The degree to which organizations will conflict is dependent one: (1) the degree to which they use different approaches and methods, and (2) the extent that resources (funding, personnel, etc.) are scarce. In community-based service delivery systems, both cooperation and conflict can occur simultaneously."

Formulating Concepts

The cognitive process of making ideas explicit produces concepts. A concept is an idea that has been consciously organized, clarified, and made into a generalization that describes a specific phenomenon—either an observable object or a nonobservable construct such as an attitude or feeling. Concepts are abstractions that encompass many fragments of reality. Put another way, a concept represents bits of reality occurring and recurring together, organized by categories and labels.

When the clinician was asked what she was studying, she replied "self-esteem." When the community organizer was asked what he was observing, he replied, "empowerment." Those two words, self-esteem and empowerment, are terms (labels) for concepts that themselves would take pages to adequately describe. When you hear the term that represents a concept, in your mind's eye you see a panorama of images representing your idea of reality. This is why we say that concepts "tap" reality. Figure 2.2 graphically represents this relationship. Concepts are abstractions that

FIGURE 2.2. Relationship between a concept and perceived reality.

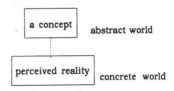

mirror the concrete world. They exist only in our minds and are the building blocks of theory.

There are many concepts embedded in Edna's ideas about the nature and dynamics of interorganizational relationships (autonomy, organization, community-based, service delivery system, etc.). She has developed some explicit ideas about effective ways to structure delivery systems, and she decides to test them starting with two concepts, cooperation and conflict.

Defining Practice Concepts

Cooperation is a means by which formal organizations deal with uncertainty. By sharing resources and joining together to accomplish agreed-upon outcomes, organizations manage environmental turbulence, solve problems, and achieve goals that no single organization acting along could solve.

Conflict can occur at many levels. Individuals, units within organizations, and organizations themselves can participate in uncooperative, hostile, and combative behavior that negatively affects the quality of service delivery.

Formulating Theories

When we describe, explain, or predict a behavior or event, we use two or more concepts bound together. This is a theory. Figure 2.3 shows this rela-

FIGURE 2.3. Relationship between concepts, theory, and perceived reality.

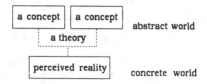

Theoretical knowledge is a grouping of ideas/concepts applicable to a relatively wide variety of circumstances. It is *generalized* knowledge. Theory, therefore, provides understanding of how the concrete world operates. When we know the nature of a social or psychological phenomenon, are aware of all its detail and facets, and can describe its structure and predict its behavior, then we have a theory. Theories are rules about behavior and assumptions about causality.

Practice theory has to be based on causal theory. When scientists observe events, they look for patterns. When they see repeating patterns, they develop ideas about what causes these patterns and generalize these ideas into causal theory. Practitioners use these general theories about the underlying nature of behavior to construct theories that predict that if a specific intervention is used, a specified behavior will change in a specified manner.

When the school social worker is asked, "How are you going to treat this child's learning disability?" and answers, "family therapy," she clearly has a causal theory made up of many ideas and assumptions about the nature of learning disabilities, the relationships between learning and family structure, and how a specific intervention will affect a child's learning processes. She has a practice theory about purposive change.

In a deductive self-assessment study, you are simply testing your causal theory about purposive change. To be able to test a theory, you

must make it explicit by decoupling the concepts in your idea and analyzing them. Ask these questions:

- What concepts are part of this idea?
- What are the definitions of these concepts?
- How do these concepts fit together into a theory that explains the behavior I'm concerned about?
- How does this theory predict that my intervention will bring about the desired change?

Edna has the components of a theory about interagency relationships.
A practitioner interested in assessing interventions could use them to construct a practice theory.

Defining Theory

Edna realized that interagency conflict and cooperation appeared to be ex-
tremes of the same phenomenon, e.g., harmony means cooperation and dis-
harmony means conflict. In fact, the literature suggested that the way to
reduce conflict in interorganizational settings was to increase cooperation and
coordination. Based on experience and her careful decoupling and defining of
these concepts, however, Edna developed a more complex causal theory:
"Conflict and cooperation in interorganizational service delivery systems exist
simultaneously and are related *positively* to one another—high levels of cooperation will often be accompanied by high levels of conflict. Interventions
that attempt to increase cooperation will not necessarily reduce conflict, but
may increase it."

FORMULATING RESEARCH QUESTIONS,
PROBLEMS, GOALS, AND HYPOTHESES

When the object of self-assessment research can be stated as explicit concepts, the next step is to construct the research design so that the theory
and concepts can be tested. To test a practice theory requires that you be
able to write a research question, name your intervention goal, and construct a hypothesis that predicts the outcome of your intervention. Your
level of specificity in naming the question, problem, and goal is dependent
upon the maturity of the intervention technology and your experience in
using the technology.

Formulating Research Questions

In order to write a research question, two decisions must be made. First, the target of the research must be selected. In other words, what is it exactly that you want to study? There are two choices. You, the practitioner, may be the object of study, or it may be the client or client system.

This choice regarding the target of study—the subject of the assessment—revolves around who it is you want to observe. If *you* are the target, you would be concerned with your behavior—whether you are using the intervention technique properly or whether some aspect of the working situation is impacting on your effectiveness. If your *client/client system* is the target, the client would be the object of study and you would study the usability and effectiveness of your intervention with that particular client/client system.

In either case the object of study is a single person or system, and data are collected concerning some aspect of functioning that is expected to change as a result of the intervention. It should be remembered that the data may come from:

- the practitioner (as when you make clinical observations of a client sequentially across time)
- the client (as when you ask an individual or members of a family to self-report behaviors)
- multiple respondents (as when you ask colleagues or employees to rate your performance on a specific task or intervention)
- multiple organizations (as when you request feedback from other agencies about your achievement on behalf of a client organization).

The second choice that must be made in order to write a research question concerns the focus of the project and pertains to *why* you decided to undertake the project. In other words, what is the purpose of your research?

If your purpose is to better understand your use of a specific intervention technology, then the research question pertains to *process* (Rosen & Proctor, 1978). Process evaluation enables you to operationally define and measure what it is you are really doing when you say you are using the xyz technique. In research language, process evaluation helps you verify your independent variable; in self-assessment research, the intervention is always the independent variable (Nelsen, 1985; Rinn & Vernon, 1985).

If the purpose is to better understand the effect of the intervention, then the question is one of *outcome*. In outcome studies you specify exactly what it is you are going to do, and then you measure the effect of the intervention on the problem (Coulton & Solomon, 1977; Mahoney, 1978; Strupp & Bloxom, 1975).

Process and outcome studies focus on very different things. Process evaluation, sometimes called formative research, looks at the application and use of technologies. Outcome evaluation, sometimes called summative research, looks at the impacts of technologies. They are both important techniques, but the use of one rather than the other depends on the maturity of the practice area.

Decisions about the target and focus of a self-assessment design are independent, meaning that there are at least four mutually exclusive ways to ask the research question. They form a four-cell typology (see Figure 2.4).

FIGURE 2.4. Typology of research questions.

	YOU	CLIENT/CLIENTSYSTEM
PROCESS	(1) Am I using this intervention the way it is supposed to be used: used? [Am I actually employing a a participative style of management?]	(2) Am I using this intervention appropriately with this type of client? [Can participative management be implemented well with this particular staff?]
OUTCOME	(3) Is this intervention affecting me in unanticipated or undesirable ways? [Is there an unexpected impact on me from using a participative management style?]	(4) Is this intervention having the desired effect on this client? [Is this participative style accomplishing what I want it to with this staff?]

Another way to conceptualize these four types of self-assessment questions is to look at what is assumed true in each condition.

- In cell one, it is assumed that the intervention technique is effective and that the client system is amenable to change. The question becomes, "Am I able to operationalize this technique and am I using it properly?"
- In cell two, it is assumed that the technique is effective. The question then becomes, "Am I able to implement this technique given the unique characteristics of this target system?"
- In cell three, it is assumed that the practitioner is using the technique properly and that it is effective with the client system. The question then becomes, "Is this technique the best one for me to use given my skills and abilities?"
- In cell four, it is assumed that the practitioner is using the technique properly and that the technique is effective, so the question becomes, "Is the technique effective with this client system?"

Because each of these assumptions of truth is subject to question, an effective self-assessment plan may include questions that address all four conditions. The important point is that any self-assessment system, if it is to be effective, must be clear, concise, and explicit in the questions it is trying to answer.

A research question is:

- A statement in the form of a question about one concept or about the relationship between two or more concepts.
- It should specify the target and focus of the research.
- It should be substantive enough that having the answer will justify the time and effort invested in obtaining it.

The importance of the research question cannot be overstated. It is a cliché to say, "you won't get the right answer unless you ask the right question" or "garbage in, garbage out." Nevertheless, these clichés are true. Assessments that tell you what you want to know, rather than something completely unrelated, start with a very careful formulation of the target and purpose of the study.

Formulating Research Questions

Edna was able to write a research question. She chose a service delivery system she was currently working with as the target, and the effect of coordination as the focus. She was able to ask the basic research question clearly, concisely, and with some degree of specificity: Does the amount of coordination in interorganizational service delivery systems have an effect on the amount of conflict that occurs? Specifically, in the Dodgeville hospice care system, can the amount of conflict be reduced by manipulating the method of coordination that is utilized?

Formulating Research Problems

The statement of a problem that is to be studied during the research process is a definition of what is. It describes the issue or issues of interest as they are, the condition that requires you to intervene. In order for you to select an intervention, you must be able to understand and explain the dysfunction. It is this picture of the situation prior to your intervention that is the statement of the problem.

Problem statements are usually not difficult to write when the client is the target of the self-assessment and you are looking at your ability to lessen the severity of the client's problem. When this is the research question, you must be careful to specify the problem in detail so that you can select the most effective intervention(s). When the target of the self-assessment is yourself, it may be more difficult to write the problem statement because the "what is" may not appear to be a problem. In this case, the problem may be a facet of your practice that causes you to feel uncertain or perplexed, or a skill or technique that you want to improve.

Regardless of the nature of the problem, it is imperative that it be specified in detail. Based on the definition of the problem, you will select an intervention and choose a means of measuring the outcome. It is quite possible to end up with information and conclusions that are not what you want and are useless because you have measured the wrong indicator with the wrong instrument—all because you did not adequately define the problem.

A research problem is:

- A statement about a current human condition that is perceived to be dysfunctional or harmful.
- It should specify indicators of the problem in concrete and measurable terms if possible.
- It should justify the problem in terms of relative seriousness and specify why solutions should be applied to it rather than to other problems.
- It should be written in the present tense.

Formulating Research Problems

After formulating the research question, Edna was able to define the problem with little effort: There is too much conflict in the hospice system as indicated by the hostility and low morale of the staff and by the fighting between the administrators. This problem is serious enough that, if it continues, interagency cooperation in serving hospice patients will decline dramatically. This is not to suggest that conflict in itself is dysfunctional, because in actuality it often leads to service improvement activities. Too much conflict, however, has severely limited this system's ability to provide high-quality care to hospice patients and their families.

Formulating Goals

If the research problem describes the condition that needs changing, then the goal describes the condition the intervention is meant to bring about. Just as it is very important to know from whence you depart theoretically, it is perhaps even more important to know your destination.

A goal is a statement about a future state of being. It should always be written as an outcome statement and should not use process words such as "becoming," "developing," or "establishing." A goal statement can describe two kinds of outcomes: (1) the conditions necessary for effective implementation of your intervention (if process evaluation), or (2) the conditions your intervention is designed to achieve (if outcome evaluation).

There is a subtle but important point here. *The goal of the research and the goal of your intervention may be very different.* If your self-assessment is focused on how well you are using the intervention, then the goals of the study are the specific skills, attitudes, and behaviors you must have to effectively implement the intervention. If the assessment is focused on your client system, then the goals of the study are the client's specific behaviors, attitudes, or feelings to be achieved before it can be said the intervention is effective.

In short, a goal is:

- A statement about what should be, a human condition perceived as being desirable and feasible.
- It should specify the expected outcome and who will display the desired behaviors, attitudes, or conditions.
- It should be written in the present or future tense.

Formulating Research Goals

Edna chose to focus on the outcomes of her work with the five organizations that make up the Dodgeville hospice care system (two hospitals, the Public Health Department, the Visiting Nurse Association, and the American Cancer Society volunteers). Her intervention was aimed at reducing the conflict between these organizations utilizing consultation and technical assistance. The goal statement, then, had to describe the hospice service delivery system in a future where conflict would be absent, or at least reduced. The goal: The Dodgeville hospice care service delivery system will operate so that hospice patients and their families receive well-planned and -executed services. There will be no fragmentation of services, and policies will be consistent, not contradictory. Administrators of member organizations will make all decisions together and will strive for consensus. Care will be provided by staff and volunteers who have all participated in the case planning, have a shared orientation to the client, and work together harmoniously. They will always have up-to-date information so that of every team it can be said, "The right hand knows what the left hand is doing."

Formulating Hypotheses

If it is possible to state with clarity the research question, the problem, and the goal, then it is time to formulate the hypothesis. This is not always possible, however. You may be able to ask the question, and you may understand the nature and cause of the problem, but at your current level of knowledge you may not be able to formulate a goal. There are self-assessment designs in Chapter 3 that you can use.

If you have been able to complete each step as outlined above, then try stating your hypothesis (Lazare, 1979). A hypothesis is an assertion about your intervention—how to solve or ameliorate the problem by using a service or treatment. The intervention (or some component of it) is the force that causes the change; it is called the independent variable (the x variable). The problem is the thing that is changed; it is known as the dependent variable (the y variable). In practice research, change in the target is attributed to, is *dependent* on, the intervention or practice technology.

Time is a fundamental concept in practice theory. Without time, we cannot study change. One snapshot, such as cross-sectional data, tells us nothing about the degree to which the target has changed from time 1 to time 2, or time 1 to time 12. It is axiomatic in systems theory that a person, group, organization, or community is never exactly the same at two points in time (Hage & Meeker, 1988). This is why we say that time series designs are essential for self-assessment research.

Time, then, underlies all hypotheses about practice, and it has an important property that must be kept in mind when constructing hypotheses: Time can go in only one direction; change can go in only one direction. In other words, the action of the cause always comes first in time. Thus, the intervention first, the effect second; if x, then y. If we know the sequence in which events occur, we know that the second can never be the cause of the first. If your client has an addiction before your intervene but not afterward, we might be able to attribute his sobriety to the success of your treatment (if we could show no other action present).

What if, you ask, the client stops drinking for a time but then resumes again? Doesn't this represent change that has gone in two directions? Yes, but in a theoretical sense we must assume that two causal processes are operating, one creating the desired change and one creating change that leads back to the original state. In this case, we must ask why the treatment was ineffective and look for the root causes of the problem because the factors that were creating the behavior in the first place have resumed their action. If the first hypothesis is not confirmed, then a second one should be constructed that seeks to explain why no change has occurred. For example, when a nonadaptive organization or a rigid family is nonresponsive to your intervention, they may be expending energy to remain always the same. You must explain why this is the case.

A hypothesis is:

- A statement about change composed of at least two concepts.
- It should use concepts that are as specific and discrete as possible.
- It should take the form of a prediction: "If x (the intervention), then y (the change that will occur)."

Formulating Hypotheses

Edna knew she was often inclined to blame administrators for the amount of conflict in interagency systems, but she couldn't really get a handle on why. She had good relationships with these people, so she talked with them individually, trying to get at what specifically would reduce the amount of conflict. What she heard in several agencies was something like this: "We know there is a lot of conflict in the hospice system, especially among the staff. That's why we developed the protocols. Everyone should know what their roles are—we have written rules that cover all contingencies. In fact, they shouldn't even have to talk with one another anymore." When she heard this, Edna realized that few administrators recognize that there are different methods of coordination. They think that the *only* way to coordinate an interagency service delivery system is to reduce the number of people making decisions (in the case of administration), or to tightly preprogram the joint work activity (in the case of staff). They believe that in this way there are no areas that can become a source of conflict. Administrators at the state level push highly formalized plans and procedures down to the community level, and community agency administrators do the same to their staffs. Edna decided that administrators in human services assume that smooth, conflict-free working relationships are achieved via less communication rather than more communication. Further, they often do not realize that conflict within service delivery systems can result from the misunderstandings and inflexibility associated with high formaliztion. Edna was then able to specify her intervention:

She was going to increase the amount of interorganizational coordination by initiating face-to-face decision making among administrators and interagency treatment teams with staff in order to reduce the amount of conflict among member agencies. The hypothesis: If the amount of face-to-face coordination among administrators and staff increases across organizational boundaries, then the amount of conflict in the system will decrease.

SELECTING DESIGNS, MEASURES, AND DATA COLLECTION METHODS

If you are using a deductive approach, selecting the design and data collection methods is the third step in the research process. If you are using an inductive approach, your self-assessment process begins here, the design of the study. Since the design (step 3) and analysis (step 4) are essentially the same regardless of your approach, we discuss them here without differentiating between them except by illustration (we continue to illustrate the deductive process with Edna's study and start an illustration of an inductive study carried out by Steve).

There is one caution, however. Deductive reasoning uses a syllogistic model such that if the premises are true, then the conclusions are true. No such model exists for inductive reasoning because when we begin with a set of observations and move to a generalization, rules cannot exist. This is called empiricism, relying solely on practical experience without regard for a system or theory. In an inductive process there is always room for others to have alternative facts and understandings of the facts.

At this point in the research process there are three major questions you must answer:

1. What type of design best fits my question and situation?
2. How will I measure the information I need?
3. From whom will I collect the information I need?

Selecting a Study Design

Until now, self-assessment research has been equated with single-subject designs. That is, most of the literature has advocated reliance on the use of quantitative time series data. These designs require that the outcome of social work interventions be specified in behavioral terms. Little attention has been given to the use of less quantitative designs.

The issue of qualitative versus quantitative designs has been loudly debated for many years. Some believe that many or most social work outcomes cannot be quantified and, therefore, that the most efficacious designs are qualitative. Others believe that only through quantitative data analysis can knowledge and theory be developed. In this guide we do not take sides in this controversy, believing instead that both types of data are essential for development of the social work profession. Because social work practice is so broad in scope, research designs must necessarily be wide-ranging.

We have chosen to discuss six designs below that represent a broad continuum from qualitative to quantitative: case study, target problem scaling, goal attainment scaling, single-system monitoring, single-system experimental designs, and multiple baseline designs. These are by no means the only designs and methods available to students and practitioners. They do, however, represent a broad spectrum of single-system research designs, and we have selected them because they are easily mastered. They are not equally appropriate for all purposes and for all settings; they are very different, and each is better for one type of self-assessment than for another.

A research design is a plan for making observations and collecting data. The design you choose will dictate the kind of data you collect, be it qualitative or quantitative, and the methods you will use to collect it. The design you choose must fit your specific situation (and the conditions of the theory, if you have one). The key to making a good decision is to determine how specific you can be about the elements of your research, given the nature of your intervention and client system.

As all social workers know, there are situations in which it is not possible to specify either the problem, the goal, or the outcomes in explicit terms. In such cases a qualitative design such as a case study is clearly preferable. At the other extreme it may be possible to be very specific about all elements; then an experimental design is desirable. The specificity requirements of each step of the research process are summarized as follows:

1. Can you clearly specify the problem(s) of concern?
2. Can you state the goal(s) of the intervention explicitly?
3. Can you specify clear behavioral outcomes that indicate progress toward the stated goal(s)?
4. Do you have a measurement tool appropriate to the goal(s)?
5. Can you explicitly describe the intervention you will use?

Table 2.1 shows the six research designs on a continuum from qualitative to quantitative and describes the minimum level of specificity necessary for each design.

TABLE 2.1. Specificity requirements of six self-assessment designs

qualitative <------------------------> quantitative

Elements	Case Study	Target Problem Scaling	Goal Attainment Scaling	Monitoring	Quasi Experimental	Multiple Baseline
Target Problem(s) Identified?	no	yes	yes	yes	yes	yes
Goal(s) Explicitly Stated?	no	no	yes	yes	yes	yes
Behavioral Outcomes Identified?	no	no	no	yes	yes	yes
Measurement Tool Required?	no	yes	yes	yes	yes	yes
Interventions Explicitly Described?	no	no	no	no	no	yes

There is some flexibility at the qualitative end of this continuum, but not at the quantitative end. For example, you could, if you wish, do a case study even though some or all of the research elements were clearly specified. Perhaps you need to expand your theory, go back and look at the total context of your client in his/her situation. In this case, you would certainly elect to do a case study. At the other end of the continuum, however, you could not use a multiple baseline design unless all of the research elements were specified. This is why we say that the design must fit the research situation: Practice situations without explicit intervention principles and theory must use qualitative designs, while highly developed areas may use highly quantitative designs. Each of these six designs represents a different approach to self-assessment.

Case study is a narrative description of an intervention. It is appropriate for situations where there is little prior research and no theory is available upon which to build the design. The outcome of a case study should be a tentative working hypothesis.

Target problem scaling is a qualitative assessment of the degree to which a presenting problem is reduced or eliminated. It is a useful design for situations where the problem is known but specificable outcomes cannot be quantified.

Goal attainment scaling is a flexible method that uses the goal statement of the intervention as the criteria and framework for the evaluation. It can be used with either qualitative or quantitative goals.

Monitoring designs use multiple measures of change in an individual client or client system over time. They require an observable and quantifiable referent for the change and the opportunity to take a minimum of seven to nine measures.

Quasi–experimental designs are similar to the monitoring design, except that they require a baseline (phase A) when the behavior or problem condition is observed prior to the intervention (phase B). The assumption is that if the problem can be observed to change during the intervention, then evidence exists to accept a causal relationship between the changing condition and the intervention. This evidence is strengthened when a complete reversal is possible; that is, the intervention is withdrawn and the condition returns to its initial level but reverses when the intervention is introduced a second time (ABAB).

Multiple baseline designs are yet another variation of the quasi experimental design. Here there are two or more baselines after which multiple interventions are introduced at the same or different times. This design can become elaborate the more rigorous the design becomes.

Selecting a Design Using an Inductive Approach

Steve Johnson has worked in the family intervention program of Support For Families (SFF) for 10 years. The majority of his work has been with families in which there has been a finding of child abuse. His job is to help the parents improve their parenting skills and to assist in the decision as to whether to place the child or children back in the home. Steve is aware that there are many theories, ideas, beliefs, rules, and regulations that are supposed to guide his practice; however, he has recently been thinking about his work and has come to realize that his actual work is guided more by his gut feelings than by any theory or even set of theories. He would probably say he uses an eclectic approach if pushed, but the truth is he really has no explicit practice theory. Steve is recognized, however, as a very effective worker within his agency and the community at large. Indeed, he is often asked to train new workers because of his skill.

Since he cannot state what he does, his research question must be, "What do I do with these families that makes my interventions successful?" He has decided to do an inductive study in order to both evaluate and better understand his practice.

One problem of abusive parents, Steve believes, is that they do not trust anyone; they will appear to comply with instructions but never actually become committed to change. His goal with every parent and child, therefore, is to establish a trusting relationship. Steve is not asking what abusive parents need; rather, he is asking what it is that he can do to help these parents trust. In other works, what is it about Steve's behavior that causes changes in these parents' behavior? Because Steve understood the problem but could not articulate his intervention, he chose to do a case study with himself as target.

Single-Family Case Study Design
  Target: Steve
  Focus: process evaluation
  Frequency of Measurement:
  1-hour interviews every week for 24 weeks

Selecting a Design Using a Deductive Approach

Edna was using a deductive process and wished to assess the effectiveness of interagency coordination as an intervention intended to control the level of conflict. In doing this self-assessment she was, of course, testing her theory about the relationship between an intervention (the independent variable) and its outcome (the dependent variable). Edna decided to use a single-system monitoring design. She asked all of the organizations that participated in the Dodgeville Hospice Coordinating Council to cooperate in her research project, and they agreed. She then had another idea. The county adjacent to Dodge had two hospice programs. One in Petersberg was going to start implementing an interagency team project; the other, in Beverly Glen, was a hospital-based system that utilized home nursing and public nursing agencies when their patients were able to be at home but had no coordinating structure. She contacted them and they were enthusiastic about the project. These three systems, she realized, would allow her to do an experimental design. She wrote:

Single-Subject Experimental Design with Multiple Baselines

> *Targets:*   *Interventions:*
>   Dodgeville Hospice (AB)   Coordinating Council (administrators)
>   Petersberg (AC)   interagency patient care teams
>   Beverly Glen (AA)   none
>
> *Focus:* outcome evaluation
>
> *Frequency of Measurement:*
>   Baseline Phases: 6 measures of conflict over 12 weeks prior to
>   implementation of Coordinating council and
>   interagency teams
>   Intervention Phase: 12 measures of conflict over 12 months after
>   implementation

OPERATIONALIZATION AND MEASUREMENT METHODS

Once you have selected a design for your assessment problem, you must operationalize your concept(s)—that is, you must decide how you will measure your intervention (the independent variable) and/or the outcome of your intervention (the dependent variable). Before you can select a measurement instrument, you must operationalize your concepts in such a way as to make them measurable.

Every research effort requires that information be captured and stored in some concrete manner. Information is captured by measuring, or describing, some facet of reality. We can never capture the totality of reality, but we can perceive some part of reality and describe it in terms of our focus or interest (e.g., a dimension, quantity, capacity, or the extent or degree of a specific attribute). The term "measurement" in research, therefore, is broad, and ranges from the identification of patterns of behavior in participant observation to the assignment of numeric values to concrete objects or indicators of an abstract condition.

An operational definition states specifically the indicator of the concept, that is, what will be measured. Indicators, or *referents* as they are called, are the links between concepts and perceived reality, the things we measure to assess change. This relationship is shown in Figure 2.5. Opera-

FIGURE 2.5. Relationship between concepts, referents, and perceived reality.

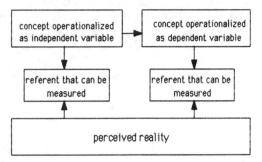

tionalization is relatively simple when the intervention or its outcome is associated with a behavior or condition that is concrete and observable. For example, the effect of a recreation program in a public housing unit may be clearly observable in terms of the number of new instances of damage and vandalism. The effect of a clinical weight reduction program is directly measurable by a bathroom scale.

When an observation must be of subjective conditions, such as intelligence, attitudes, beliefs, or customs, measurement becomes more difficult because these conditions do not have shape or substance that makes them directly measurable. In this case, we must find an indicator that represents the abstract condition. We cannot directly measure a feeling or attitude; we can only measure what we can observe. Substitutes must be found for these nonconcrete conditions and intervention effects. These proxies may be:

- a specific activity or set of activities. With this type of referent we make an inference from a directly observed behavior. For example, we measure affection by observing the number of times a parent hugs a child.

- a statement. With this type of referent we make an inference directly from what we hear. For example, we hear a parent tell us how many times they hugged their child.
- a score on a test or scale. With this type of referent we infer an attitude, feeling, or belief from a text or scale score. For example, a parent completes a pencil and paper test designed to estimate the ability to nurture and show his/her children affection.

Operationalizing Concepts Using an Inductive Approach

Steve was a Family Development Specialist with the Joslin Midtown Community Action Program (CAP). This CAP was in the midst of implementing a new program for low-income families, the purpose of which was to reduce welfare dependency and increase self-sufficiency.

Steve was assigned to work in the Income Maintenance Office of the County Department of Human Services (DHS). The reason for locating him in the DHS office was so that he could do intakes with young families who were first-time applicants for AFDC and offer them the opportunity to participate in the Family Development Program. The objectives of the intake interview were, of course, broader than merely information and referral, but Steve knew that assessment of his effectiveness would be based solely on the number of families who enrolled in the Family Development Program.

What Steve needed to know was how to do an AFDC intake interview so that it motivated young single mothers (90% of the intakes) to participate in this program. He thought he could accomplish this objective—that is why he volunteered for the job. He knew also that his confidence was based on the fact that he worked with clients using an unconscious theory of how to do it. He decided, therefore, to do a process-oriented self-assessment with himself as the target in order to formulated the concepts that would specify the major components of this intervention intake. Steve could not, of course, operationalize these concepts at this point in the development of this program. That is why he chose an inductive approach.

Operationalizing Concepts Using a Deductive Approach

Because Edna was working from an explicit theory, her concepts were already operationally defined in the literature. Edna wrote:

Coordination: Coordination is a method of harmonizing service delivery involving two or more organizations. Coordination of administrators is achieved through decision-making structures that can be classified as *impersonal, personal,* or *group*. Coordination of staff is achieved through task integration methods that can be classified as *independent, reciprocal,* or *collective*. The more face-to-face communication that occurs, the more feedback there is, and therefore the more coordination there will be. Thus, group decision making and collective task integration provide more coordination than do impersonal and independent methods (Thompson, 1967; Van de Ven, Delbecq, & Koening, 1976; Van de Ven & Ferry, 1980).

Conflict: Interagency conflict is a dimension of interaction between the staffs of autonomous organizations. Conflict can range from disputes and disagreements to contests and open warfare. Conflict can occur covertly or overtly, and it can be represented by verbal communication or direct actions.

It is most important that concepts be operationalized such that referents will accurately represent the focus or interest. Edna, when she operationalizes coordination as administrative decision-making structures and staff task integration methods, is using referents that have been proven reliable by other researchers. When Steve thought about the focus of his study, he realized he could not indentify useful concepts, so, of course, he could not operationalize them. Operational definitions of his concepts and a hypothesis linking them together will be the outcome of his study.

When the indicator is directly representative, then the measure is said to be valid. In general, validity is high when an instrument is good at measuring what it purports to measure. Most statistical textbooks give methods for assessing validity. For our purposes, a measure or indicator must have an identifiable and clear link to the object, behavior, or attitude we specify we are measuring. If a test purports to measure self-esteem, it must yield a higher score for those individuals who appear very self-confident than for those who appear less self confident.

A measure must also be reliable. That is, it must yield about the same score under the same conditions at various points in time. Again, statistical texts give several techniques for assessing reliability. For our purposes, the measure selected must show the same relationship to the item of interest whenever we apply the measure under the same conditions. If the measure changes over time regardless of the intervention, then we have no way of assessing whether the intervention had any impact.

There are two other issues concerning measurement and instruments that are important to keep in mind. The first is that some instruments are highly reactive. A measure is said to be reactive when the instrument itself alters the item being measured. The mere fact that you ask a client to record the number of cigarettes she/he smokes may change the smoking behavior. If you suspect that your measure is reactive, use multiple measures or measures of which the client is not aware.

The second issue is that of tautology, circular reasoning that leads us to measure the wrong thing. Suppose the client's problem is overweight, and she/he chooses to lose weight by dieting. Very often the person will define dieting as losing weight and losing weight as dieting—the intervention and the outcomes are one. The problem is that a measured weight loss may come from a number of sources such as illness, exercise, or depression, causes that have nothing to do with dieting. To avoid this problem, it is necessary to clearly specify different independent and dependent variables in order to measure the correct variable. In this case the intervention could be specified as a diet that is dependent on fewer calories being consumed, minutes of aerobic exercise performed, and days lived without snacking. Having multiple outcome indicators can also help avoid tautology.

Selecting Measurement Instruments

When you have operationalized the concepts so that you know clearly and in detail how they will be measured, then you are ready to select a measurement instrument. The range of measurement tools that can be used in self-assessment research is very broad indeed. Some you may construct yourself:

1. *Observation protocols* used in conjunction with video- or audio-tape capture events and occurrences. You record the totality of activity and then extract relevant portions using the protocol as a guide. This is the most qualitative of all the methods for describing behavior.
2. *Logs and journals* are written records of events, interactions, thoughts, and feelings. They are notes that focus on specific problems and/or goals and may be analyzed by content analysis. They may be very formal or briefly jotted. They are an excellent means of sorting data in case studies where the aim is to generate ideas and theory (Bloom & Fischer, 1982; Burrill, 1975).
3. *Protocols* are written items that serve as a guide for observation. In the case of naturalistic observation, they may be lists of concepts on which to concentrate or lists of questions to ask in inter-

views (Glaser & Strauss, 1967). Although observation and the use
of protocols have been a field research technique for many years
(Johnson & Bolstad, 1973; Kent & Foster, 1979), they are currently also being used in clinical settings (Jones, Reid, & Patterson, 1975).

4. *Survey questionnaires* are paper forms containing questions con-
    structed to obtain data on attitudes, beliefs, and opinions of sub-
    jects. The items may be closed- or open-ended. The items may be
    written so that each measures one concept, or multiple items may
    be aggregated as a measure of one concept (Berdie & Anderson,
    1974). Questionnaires may be administered through the mail, over
    the phone, or in personal interviews (Fink & Kosecoff, 1985).

5. *Behavioral measures* require that behaviors or behavioral indica-
    tors be stated with specificity. There are several behavior-count-
    ing techniques available, but there are no standardized behavior
    scales—the practitioner must develop a report form specifically
    for each type of observation (Behling & Merves, 1984; Bellack &
    Hersen, 1977). Behavioral measures can be used in either process
    or outcome research regardless of the target. All that is required is
    that the behavior be specified in quantifiable terms. These may be
    simple counts of behaviors, counts of behaviors within specific
    time frames, or percentages of behaviors related to opportunities
    to show the behavior (Walls, Werner, Bacon, & Zane, 1977;
    Webb, Campbell, Schwartz, & Sechrest, 1981). A list of behav-
    ioral outcome measures can be found in Appendix B.

Self-assessment instruments are used in research situations when your data
collection needs are usually very unique. There are many situations, however, when instruments have already been created that are suitable for
your purpose:

6. *Standardized instruments* utilize paper and pencil to obtain data
    that can be quantified. They have been constructed by researchers
    to measure attitudes and feelings (e.g., depression, marital satis-
    faction, self-esteem) and are readily available and fairly easy to
    administer and score. An annotated bibliography of psychosocial
    measures is in Appendix C. The primary advantage of stan-
    dardized scales is that they are normed for specific subpopulations
    of clients. They may serve as the data collection method for any
    design in which the client is the target, and the focus is the out-
    come of the intervention. In recent years several books of scales
    suitable for social work practice have been published: Hudson
    (1981) has developed a set of scales for measuring clinical prob-

lems, and Corcoran and Fischer (1987) have collected several other clinical scales. In using standardized scales it is important to determine that the validity and reliability of the scale have been established for the population for which you are using it.

Selecting Measurement Instruments Using an Inductive Approach

Steve video-taped his first two interviews and studied them closely. After several viewings it became clear to him that he followed the same process in both intakes. He: (1) established trust, (2) indicated unqualified acceptance of the client, (3) validated his clients' worth, (4) challenged their perceptions of themselves, (5) encouraged goal setting (a future not on AFDC), (6) explained the Family Development Program, and (7) established the idea that the clients, if they accepted the offer, would be entering into an equal partnership with workers in the program.

This conceptualization of the interview process enabled Steve to develop an instrument to use when observing what he increasingly thought of as a Nurturing Interview.

Assessment of Nurturing Interview

	Not at All		Fully
The interviewer . . .			
established rapport and trust	1 2 3 4 5 6 7 8 9		
indicated genuine acceptance of client	1 2 3 4 5 6 7 8 9		
validated clients' worth	1 2 3 4 5 6 7 8 9		
challenged clients' perception of self-worth	1 2 3 4 5 6 7 8 9		
encouraged goal setting	1 2 3 4 5 6 7 8 9		
explained the Family Development Program	1 2 3 4 5 6 7 8 9		
established reality of equal partnership			

	Not at All		Fully
The client(s) . . .			
indicated trust in the interviewer	1 2 3 4 5 6 7 8 9		
indicated genuine acceptance of interviewer	1 2 3 4 5 6 7 8 9		
accepted validation of his/her worth	1 2 3 4 5 6 7 8 9		
indicated change in perception of self-worth	1 2 3 4 5 6 7 8 9		
accomplished goal setting	1 2 3 4 5 6 7 8 9		
understood the Family Development Program	1 2 3 4 5 6 7 8 9		
accepted idea of equal partnership	1 2 3 4 5 6 7 8 9		

Selecting Measurement Instruments Using a Deductive Approach

Because she had to take 18 measures, Edna knew she would have to have a simple method for measuring conflict. She also knew, given the nature of her target, that she would have to use a questionnaire. She decided to write one item, have it printed on a prestamped postcard, and ask respondents to drop it in the mail.

Edna's item:

- On an average, how many times per week do the following occur while you are interacting or working with (staff) (administrators) from other agencies in your service delivery system:

	Number of Times
you have angry feelings toward another (team)(council) member?	_____
you have a verbal dispute with another (team)(council) member?	_____
you act covertly (behind the back)	
to neutralize another member?	_____
to exclude another member?	_____
to injure another member?	_____
you act overtly	
to neutralize another member?	_____
to exclude another member?	_____
to injure another member?	_____

Selecting Observers and Collecting Data

At the same time you select a measurement instrument, you must decide from whom you will collect the information you need. There is a misconception concerning the source of information for self-assessment research. Just because the target of the research is a single person or system, this does not mean that the source of the assessment information has to be a single person. We believe that using multiple persons as observers is not only appropriate, but increases the validity of your conclusions. In general, data collected by someone other than the subject of investigation is considered more objective and hence more valid. There are four major sources of information:

1. *Clients and client systems* are the most obvious. As noted above, asking clients to make and record observations of themselves tends to heighten awareness and clarify problems. This is true in organizational and community settings as well as in clinical practice.

2. *Outside expert consultation* is a valid and very useful tool. Consultants are most often used in process evaluation when the focus is operationalizing an intervention or judging your use of an intervention. A consultant may use any of the other methods described above or many simply serve as an independent observer. The primary advantage of utilizing a consultant is that he/she, as an independent observer, helps remove any in-house bias. Under these conditions, the consultant brings validity to the evaluation design as well as fulfilling a coaching and teaching function. The primary disadvantage of consulting as a method of feedback is that consultants are frequently expensive.

3. *Peer review* is not often thought of as a source of data for self-assessment, but it can be a very effective means of evaluating your own performance and interventions (Chernesky & Young, 1979). Clinical workers often voluntarily seek advice from colleagues within their own work units during formal staffings and informal discussions. Administrators and community organizers, on the other hand, seldom do. Perhaps this is because they fear losing their colleagues' confidence or because they are reluctant to risk loss of status. The fact is, however, that those we work with— clients, staff, volunteers, other administrators—have unique and relevant perceptions of our performances and are a most valuable source of feedback. Practitioners truly interested in self-improvement will not ignore the contributions that peers can make in this endeavor.

4. *Yourself.* As discussed in Chapter 1, there are situations where you must be the source of self-assessment data. If you are doing a process evaluation (looking at your behavior or feelings during the treatment process) or an outcome evaluation (looking at the intervention's effect upon yourself), then you may have to collect information from yourself to include in the study's findings.

It should be noted that whenever data can be collected from multiple sources, then the design is strengthened and the results will be more reliable. This is especially true when you are the target of study; you should always find another source against which to test your perceptions.

Selecting Sources of Information Using an Inductive Approach

Steve knew that by videotaping himself he was collecting information from himself. He knew also that he would use the tapes to describe explicitly the behaviors that constitute his relationship-building intervention. He would therefore need another source of information to verify his observations.

Steve asked his co-workers in the Family Development Program to observe 12 tapes—1 interview per week for 12 weeks—scoring each with the instrument he developed (to do this, of course, required permission from the participants). By using peer review Steve was not only seeking assessment of his performance, but he was also using the process as a program development tool.

Steve waited several months and then collected information on all the AFDC applicants that he had seen in intake interviews. Of the 62 clients for which he had outcome data, 25 had agreed to participate in the program. When he compared these results with how his co-workers had reviewed the tapes, he realized that with these 25 clients he had been given the highest scores on building rapport and trust and challenging applicants' self-perception. Moreover, these clients were judged as having the highest level of trust in Steve. He concluded, therefore, that the two most important components of a Nurturing Interview are trust and challenge, and he hypothesized that when they are accomplished clients will be more likely than not to participate in the Family Development Program.

Selecting Sources of Information Using a Deductive Approach

Edna had only to decide how many respondents she would need for her study. One thing was obvious: it would be administrators in Dodgeville and staff persons in Petersberg . . . but then she had a thought. It could be that if conflict was reduced at one level it might subside at another level. In other words, if the Coordinating Council succeeded in lowering conflict in the Dodgeville hospice program among the administrators, maybe conflict among staff would also go down—and vice versa in Petersberg. Thinking that this was a rather intriguing extension of her theory, Edna decided to collect data from all administrators and staff involved in the hospice programs in the three communities. Further, she decided that she would administer the first questionnaire personally at each Coordinating Council meeting in Dodgeville, all interagency team meetings in Petersberg, and all individual administrators and workers in Beverly Glen. This would give her an opportunity to explain the purpose and timetable for the study and motivate her subjects to return the questionnaires. Thereafter she would mail the participants the question-naire at the time she needed it completed and ask that they complete it and return it immediately.

LAST BUT MOST IMPORTANTLY

When you have completed the research design, you are not yet ready to collect your data. It is at this point that you must consider the rights and protection of those from whom you are collecting data.

Whenever you are using human subjects, there are ethics that man-date certain policies and procedures. Any institution receiving federal re-search funds must have an institutional review board to which you must apply for permission to do research under the auspices of that institution (see Appendix F for a sample human subjects review application). If your agency or organization does not have a review board as such, it may have a research committee that reviews and approves research carried on under its sponsorship. At a minimum, you should have your supervisor's approval for any research involving human subjects. This is true even if you are the subject.

There are three major rules that guide the protection of human sub-jects. First, all research must be evaluated in terms of its potential short- and long-term risk to those involved. Risk is defined as any experience that produces anxiety, discomfort, embarrassment, or frustration beyond the levels normally expected in everyday life. Research that may put respon-dents or subjects at risk for these effects beyond a minimal level must be evaluated by a institutional review board or its equivalent.

The second principle is that subjects must give their *informed consent*. Informed consent is defined as a situation where the subject has had a full and fair explanation of the procedures to be followed and the nature of the research and understands any risks associated with the research. Subjects must also understand that they can withdraw from the research at any time without prejudice to themselves or their families.

Third, it is incumbent upon the researcher to take reasonable steps to protect the confidentiality of subjects' records. This means that you must assure that you have done all in your power to protect the records from disclosure and have a plan to notify subjects if confidentiality is somehow breached.

If you have any questions about the ethics of a research project it is very important that you resolve these prior to beginning the project. If you, your supervisor, and/or your agency cannot resolve an ethical issue, it is wise to obtain help from another institution that has an institutional review board.

3 Qualitative Designs

Included in this chapter and the next are single-system designs employed for the purpose of self-assessment. The examples in this chapter use three of the qualitative designs presented in Chapter 2—case studies, target problem scaling, and goal attainment scaling—and apply them to both micro and macro practice across diverse fields of social work practice. These self-assessments are equally divided between designs with clients and practitioners as targets, and they are balanced between process and outcome evaluations.

The purpose of these examples is to demonstrate how to choose the most useful research design given a specific context and focus. You may read through these 12 illustrations even though we have not yet taken you through step four—analyzing your data. Or you may want to familiarize yourself with the material in Chapter 5 on reducing qualitative data before you read these cases. We also want to suggest that one's imagination is the only limit to the use of these methodologies for improving the quality of social work practice. Although we have tried to write useful and plausible examples, they are not intended to be descriptive clinical case studies because space does not permit that level of detail.

CASE STUDIES

As social workers we are often confronted with problems or situations that are not clear and in which we simply do not have a theory or enough information to form a hypothesis. When confronted with a new situation or an unfamiliar one, forming a hypothesis too early may lead to erroneous or unproductive understandings of the situation (M. M. Wolf, 1978). In these cases it is best to use a case study design (Yin, 1984).

A case study involves gathering large amounts of information about the client/client system of interest and describing it in as much detail as possible. In conducting this type of research the practitioner remains as objective as possible and simply collects a wide range of information about the system of interest. While specific tests may be used as a part of the information-gathering process, the researcher is more likely to use observation, interviews, and existing records in a less structured format (Kagle, 1984). Practitioners may also use consultants or peers to do studies of their use of specific intervention techniques (Compton & Galaway, 1979).

This approach is usually inductive and moves from data to observed relationships to theories and hypotheses. Once the data are collected, the researcher summarizes it by use of categories. In the analysis phase the researcher looks for relationships and repetitive patterns that occur within the system and between this and other systems. It is often from this type of research that hypotheses are formed that are later subjected to more rigorous research.

Elements Required

Problem Statement?	No. Case study starts from an observational position. In this approach the interest is in describing; however, the researcher may be interested in describing relationships in a specific problem area.
Goal Statement?	No. Case study does not require a goal statement. A goal may define the area of interest.
Observable Outcomes?	No. This approach is open and requires no previous statement of expected outcomes.
Measurement Tool?	No. This approach requires no specific measurement tool. The emphasis is on describing. There are many ways of recording and storing data, such as logs and audio and visual tapes.
Intervention Methods?	No. This technique may be used to determine what intervention is appropriate and to describe processes and events that occur while applying a given technique, but it is applicable to all techniques.

Multipurpose Design?   Yes. This design may be used as the methodology
                        to assess process or outcomes and may monitor
                        both client and practitioner behavior.
Reliability and   It is very difficult to assess reliability and validity
Validity?   of case study approaches. These concepts are
                        really not applicable to inductive designs. The
                        more pertinent criteria are concerned with
                        accuracy and utility of the recording—questions
                        that can be addressed by the use of expert super-
                        vision and consultation.

Directions for Doing Case Studies

This design may consist of jotted notes about a client or area of interest to
very elaborate recordings of interviews and the use of standardized testing.

1. Select the target of the investigation.
2. Select the methods by which information will be gathered, that is,
    recorded observations, interviews, process recording.
3. Gather the data in as neutral a way as possible.
4. Write a description of the subject paying particular attention to
    relationships and repetitive patterns in the data.
5. Form hypotheses about the observed phenomenon.

---

*Sally is on the social work staff of a mental health center and is
forced to design and initiate a system of self-assessment. She
chooses to begin with a process-focused case study with herself
as target.*

Sally Johnson is a case worker at a mental health center who has just been
informed by the director that she must begin to use self-assessment techniques. Sally asked her supervisor what exactly was needed and how she was
to go about developing an evaluation system. She argued that she did intensive therapy and used an eclectic approach and therefore saw no way to evaluate what she did. The evaluation systems she had seen assumed a specific
approach to therapy and required that specific outcomes be measured. She
stated that she knew of no measure of human growth—her measure of outcome effectiveness.

    After much discussion with her supervisor, Sally decided to use a case
study approach with herself as the target. A case study was her choice because
she realized she could not specify in any detail either the independent variable
(what she did) or the dependent variable (what changes she sought for her
clients). She made herself the subject because she wanted to study her own
performance as opposed to her clients' behavior. The hope was that patterns

would begin to emerge from Sally's work that would indicate what she did with clients and which of her interventions seemed to lead to the changes she desired to help her clients make.

Sally knew that no standardized data collection instrument was appropriate to her task; consequently, she decided to use clinical observations to gather data about her performance. Sally videotaped two sessions per week, which were used to describe what Sally and her clients did in these sessions. The first observer was the supervisor; she simply listed the clinical events as they occurred. The second observer was Sally herself; at the end of every therapy session she wrote a process recording of what occurred, her response to the event, and a brief explanation of why the event occurred. The goal was to record as accurately as possible what actually happened in Sally's sessions with her clients.

Supervisor's Recording of Events

S   Greets client. Asks about recent ball game and whether client was pleased with the score.
C   Satisfied with score. Mentions hot weather.
S   Comments on weather and asks how things have gone on the job.
C   Is fairly happy with the week on the job but has had some real problems with wife.
S   Asks for specific details of interactions with wife.
C   Gives several details about wife. Says wife tried to pick fights all week.
S   Asks client to be more specific about a single situation.
C   Tells about last Saturday. Wife wanted him to mow lawn while he wanted to watch ball game. Nagged him all afternoon so he couldn't enjoy game.
S   Asks how client reacted.
C   Tried to ignore her, told her to shut up, threatened to hit her, refused to mow lawn.
S   Asks how client feels about both his and his wife's behavior.
C   Discusses feelings at length. Felt humiliated and is angry with self.

Excerpts from Sally's Process Recording

Event	My response	Explanation
Client had fight with wife	Am angry; have told him to avoid fighting	Didn't make my prescription clear
Client began to realize that he precipitated fight	Glad he is beginning to accept responsibility for problem	Insight developed when he talked about his feelings of disappointment

An inspection of both sets of data revealed that Sally tended to divide her sessions into three segments: the socialization section, the work section, and the wrap-up section. Sally and her supervisor further observed that Sally tended to communicate with her clients primarily through questions during the first two sections and with statements during the wrap-up. A time study indicated that Sally spent 3 to 5 minutes on socialization, about 40 minutes on work, and another 3 to 5 minutes on wrap-up. An analysis of her questions indicated that socialization questions tended to be fairly superficial and were not designed to elicit information but rather to put the clients at ease and to communicate "I'm glad to see you" messages. Work questions were designed to elicit factual information, perceptions, feelings, and client ideas and plans. Wrap-up statements tended to be summative or prescriptive.

Further, they observed that work questions tended to elicit the most information from clients when the socialization section had effectively put them at ease. Clients responded best when Sally followed a fact–perception–feeling–plan process of questioning. In those cases where Sally skipped one or more steps, the clients appeared to get confused and to do little therapeutic work. Finally, the supervisor pointed out that prescriptive statements tended to be followed (as based on client reports at the next session) only when Sally had done a large amount of feeling and planning questioning during the work section.

Based on their assessment of these observations, Sally and her supervisor hypothesized that Sally was most effective with her clients when she followed the fact–perception–feeling–plan sequence of questioning. The next assessment Sally designed tested this hypothesis to see if indeed Sally followed this sequence independent of the particular therapy model she was using.

> *John is a youth worker with a problem that he cannot define. He does a case study of the outcome of his group work with himself as target.*

John Morrison works for Teen Times, a local organization that works with problem teenagers. His work is varied; he does conjoint family therapy, individual counseling, advocacy, and group work. His groups are for 12- to 14-year-olds who have been referred by the schools as being at high risk for substance abusers. The groups are educational and reflective and are designed to help teens clarify their own and their families' beliefs and values regarding the use and abuse of chemicals. John has three separate groups that meet twice a week and that have been running for about 5 years.

John is feeling burned out. He can't identify any particular problem; the job has just become less fun. Before deciding to look for another job, he decided to evaluate the situation to determine if there was something he could change that would restore his interest in working with teens.

After thinking through the situation, he decided that the kids in his groups haven't changed very much, the psychological rewards are still satisfactory, and the pay is decent. Viewed objectively the job is exactly the kind of job he wanted, and if he decided to move, he would probably look for a similar kind of job. But his question remained: Why am I so unhappy in this position?

John talked with his wife, his supervisor, and several friends and realized that his dissatisfaction was somehow related to the substance abuse prevention groups. He thought this an interesting idea because in this area of his practice—his group work—he could specify the independent variable in great detail. The groups meet for an hour a week for 12 weeks, and there is a specific agenda for each group meeting. The groups are structured such that one week involves a factual presentation about some facet of substance use and abuse and the next week involves discussion about what that area means to group members. Since the teens in the groups seem to respond well and the school and parents are well satisfied with the effect the groups are having (as indicated by his outcome evaluations), John decided that he must be the target of the assessment. What he wanted to know was: How are these groups impacting me? In other words, John could not specify an dependent variable in regard to himself. He wanted to know: What is happening to me?

Because he was interested in what impact these groups were having on himself, John decided to gather information about himself from himself. This decision was based upon the idea that somehow these groups were having a very strong negative impact, but one that probably would not be apparent to an outside observer. The evaluation forms that the participants fill out at the end of each 12-week session are usually very positive, and those who had come from other agencies and communities to observe John's groups always seemed to be impressed with his work. Whatever was happening internally, it was not apparent to an external observer.

To gather information about his problem, John decided to keep a journal in which he would write after each group session. He divided it into three parts. Part One was a summary of what happened in the group. He noted who was in attendance, what was discussed, and his observations about group process. Part Two was a journal in which he recorded his feelings and level of comfort or discomfort with the group session. Part Three was a relational journal in which he recorded specific events that seemed to trigger strong reactions in himself.

John kept the journal for 12 weeks. During this time he had one group that started and ended in phase with his journal, a group that went for the last 6 weeks and then the first 5 weeks of a new group, and the last 2 weeks of a group and the first 7 weeks of the next group. In all, he had entries for 32 group sessions.

Factual Journal
Group # 4 Session # 5
Present: Jim J., Sally M., Billy S., Bob N., Judy Y., and Carol L. Discussion of presentation on your right to choose and your right to be trusted. Group went well. Carol reluctant to participate at first but later got very involved. Billy and Sally engaged in less goofing off than usual.

Affective Journal
Group # 1 Session # 2
Generally comfortable with the group tonight for the first half hour.

Grew more and more uncomfortable near the end. When Sam related the fight with his father over listening to heavy metal, I wanted to scream. What trivial things kids choose to fight about!

Relational Journal

Group # 6 Session # 8

Carol told the group about a fight with her mother over what clothes she could wear to school. The group generally felt that Carol had a right to choose her own wardrobe. I noticed a feeling of discomfort when the discussion started that intensified as the group got further and further into their rights to make their own decisions.

John first analyzed his data by identifying the sequence of events from the factual journal and plotting his feelings against this sequence. From these data, he determined that there was no relationship between his feelings and the time or order of the groups, who was present at the groups, or the particular subject matter of the group. He studied journal three. He wrote a list of events in the group that triggered strong feelings in him. Here a pattern emerged. Whenever anyone in the group began to discuss the issue of separating their values from their parents' values, John had strong reactions. He was startled by this insight because he saw himself as "a very together person" and believed that he had resolved his separation from his parents.

In the hope of unravelling what was happening in his life, John shared these findings with a colleague from another agency. As they discussed why he had such a strong reaction to the group members discussing their differences with their parental value systems, they discovered that John was not concerned about his relationship with his parents and had indeed dealt adequately with it. What became apparent was that John was concerned about his relationship with his daughter, who was then 12 and beginning to show the first signs of adolescent rebellion. When John used this information to focus on this issue, he found that his sense of job satisfaction returned.

> *Sheila is the administrator of a neighborhood development program and is having trouble working with her Board of Directors. To find out what is wrong, she does a process evaluation with herself as target.*

Sheila is the director of Friendly House, a settlement house and neighborhood development agency in a deteriorating section of a large midwestern city. This is the first top administrative position she has had and she has been here for about 2 years. Friendly House is a large multiservice organization with three divisions: family services, outreach and casework, and advocacy. On the whole Sheila feels she has grown into doing administrative work and feels confident that she is doing a good job.

Friendly House depends on the local community for 85% of its funding (the only other funds are the subsidized lunch program and the federal commodities program). Sheila knows that her agency is only as strong as the support it receives from its environment—neighborhood residents, governmental officials, and influential friends. Because of this conviction she has worked very hard to build this support, one method being the reestablishment of a strong and active Board of Directors. Members of the Board are drawn from each of the three major constituencies.

In spite of her overall feeling of confidence, Sheila begins to notice that as Board meeting day approaches she becomes tense and nervous. She realizes that she dreads these meetings! Why should this be so? "Why should Board meetings be so stressful for me?" she asks herself.

Sheila decided to take time out and examine herself, to step back from the crunch of everyday work in order to study her anxiety. She designs a self-assessment with the following elements: First, since she doesn't understand clearly what the problem is, her self-assessment is process- rather than outcome-oriented. She, of course, is the target, and the research question would be, "Why am I feeling so anxious about Board meetings? Is it because I'm not conducting these meetings the way I want to conduct them?" These elements—process evaluation without a clear notion of either the intervention or the outcome—mean she must do a case study. A case study of herself would allow her to analyze the methods she currently uses during meetings and from that analysis determine what it is about her performance that is troubling her.

As a start, she tape records the next meeting and then stays home for a day to write out a process recording of what transpired (Figure 3.1).

FIGURE 3.1. Excerpt from Sheila's process recording of a board meeting.

Board Members	Sheila	Sheila's Reaction
R. Lupez: ..but you said the day care program will serve only children of working parents.		Oh, here they go again, how can I stop this?
T. Jones: No she didn't. That's only if the goal is self-sufficiency...		
	Tom Jones is right but...	
H. Higgins: No buts. As Treasurer of this agency I want to say right here and now we can't run a day care program without client fees.		Hilliary Higgins is not even understanding the issue
	Hilliary, we're not talking about financing right now.	
S. Cruz: No, we are talking about eligibility and I think it's crucial that we have an open door policy.		
	But Sheldon, universal access will mean that we will have to drop another service.	Oh dear, we talking about costs!
R. Lupez: I move we table this proposal until we have more information.		Another delay!

This process recording gave Sheila an idea about the cause of her problem. She had a good intellectual understanding of planning, and she had worked as an urban planner for 5 years, but during this time she had not had to "sell" her plans to decision makers—they were always presented by the city administrator to the city council. Sheila drew two specific conclusions from the process recording. First, Board members were not focusing on the essentials of her proposal. Their dialogue seemed diffuse and disorganized, which contributed to the inability of members to make up their minds. They just kept talking and talking, with the conversation going nowhere. Second, because the members seemed unable to grasp the core of the plan, they argued unnecessarily because of misunderstandings, which caused Sheila to "oversell" the proposal in an effort to control the confusion.

With this diagnosis of the problem, Sheila did some reading and talked with several colleagues whose ability to run effective meetings she admired. It became clear that in an attempt to fully involve all her members and ensure that they be able to make informed decisions, she was overwhelming them with unnecessary details and extraneous minutiae. Sheila decided that she could improve the method she used to present proposals at her Board meetings. Her goal became as follows:

> I must enable my Board members to focus on my vision, what I consider important. This requires simplicity, not complexity. When I present a plan or proposal I will clearly and concisely answer four questions: (1) What is the proposal? (2) Why am I recommending it? (3) What are its goals? (4) How much will it cost to implement? Prior to the meeting, each member will receive a briefing paper that answers these questions in no more than four pages.

Sheila implemented this method of presenting proposals. In order to evaluate whether she was indeed able to be concise and to present a plan in a more focused way, she asked her two colleagues to act as consultants, to attend meetings to observe her performance and critique it for her. To aid them in focusing their observations, she prepared an observation protocol (Figure 3.2).

Sheila embarked on an iterative process in which she used the specific feedback she received to improve her presentation skills and then tested herself by asking the consultants to observe her again. Three iterations of this process brought her to a point where she felt much more self-confident, and the knot in her stomach was absent as meeting days approached.

John is supervisor of outpatient clinical services and has a staff problem he is trying to manage. He does a process evaluation with the staff as target.

John has just taken over as supervisor. He has been warned that there is a wide division among the staff that often results in protracted bickering. The factions are identified as "the behaviorists" and "the psychoanalytically oriented" therapists. He knows he has a problem on his hands, one that could

FIGURE 3.2. Friendly House board meeting observation protocol.

Friendly House Board Meeting Observation Protocol

Please assess my performance in presenting plans and proposals to the Board. My objectives are to:

Summarize my proposal simply, but with adequate detail

Indicators of effectiveness: Indicators of ineffectiveness:

_____   _____
_____   _____
_____   _____

Present my rationale for the plan concisely and convincingly

Indicators of effectiveness: Indicators of ineffectiveness:

_____   _____
_____   _____
_____   _____

Explain the goal(s) by means of graphs representing summary data

Indicators of effectiveness: Indicators of ineffectiveness:

_____   _____
_____   _____
_____   _____

Make clear the resources needed to implement the proposal

Indicators of effectiveness: Indicators of ineffectiveness:

_____   _____
_____   _____
_____   _____

jeopardize the quality of patient services, but he does not have a clue about what to do about it. He has always employed a consultative model of supervision, but he is worried that this will not work well with a combative and uncooperative staff.

Although John could easily choose an indicator of outcome effectiveness for this problem, such as a reduction in verbal bickering and backstabbing, he decides not to do an outcome evaluation. Rather, he decides to do an assessment of his ability to adapt his consultative style to this group. To do this he must understand the causes of the problem and find ways of managing it. This means a process evaluation with his staff as target.

Because John wants to operate from a factual basis, he starts keeping notes in a journal. His journal includes notes that focus on the communication dynamics of the staff. After studying his journal for the first 6 weeks, he realizes that there is a definite pattern to the conflict that erupts in staff meetings. To verify this observation, he develops a schedule for analyzing his journal notes (Figure 3.3).

This analysis of the journal produced some insights. Conflicts usually developed during case reviews, usually between the two senior staff members, Jan, a behaviorist, and Hal, an analyst. The conflict was usually over appropri-

FIGURE 3.3. John's schedule for analyzing staff meeting notes.

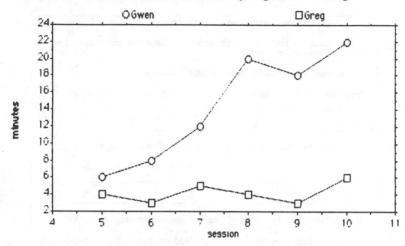

ate treatment strategy and symptom substitution. Further, he was able to see that all of his attempts to arbitrate these disputes during staff meetings only served to increased the severity of the problem. John decided not to play the arbitration role. He noted that Jan and Hal were highly successful in projecting to their audience and consolidated control over their followers through the dispute/arbitration process, and he therefore decided not to sanction it with his participation. He decided rather to let the situation escalate, but to bring the two together outside of staff meetings.

John told Jan and Hal that he was impressed with their clinical skills, their willingness to teach and assist other staff, and their ability to defend their respective perspectives. He said, however, that he felt their effectiveness as senior staff was being diminished by incessant arguing and that his supervisory effectiveness was threatened. He said that he wanted to maintain a collegial atmosphere, but it required a certain degree of cooperation, trust, and tolerance for opposing views. Then he read portions of his journal to them. He told them that he certainly understood the need to defend one's professional insights, but suggested that there was no one best way to develop a treatment plan. He then instructed them to make their own process recordings of the conflicts that occurred in staff meetings.

Over the next several months the three met periodically to give each other feedback. Though both Jan and Hal often tried to engage John in a struggle, he remained neutral and insisted that they handle their differences between themselves. Although Jan and Hal never became a harmonious team, they did become an effective team, using their different beliefs about client change to challenge each other, to clarify concepts, and, therefore, to improve their clinical work.

John felt that his self-assessment gave him an opportunity to solve his supervisory problem and to assess his effectiveness. He felt that his notes were

a help in understanding the problem and then later in monitoring his management of it. He felt the notes indicated that he had brought the conflict under
control without having to take sides and without harming the status of the staff
involved.

TARGET PROBLEM SCALING

Target problem designs are a qualitative approach to self-assessment. They
require the practitioner to identify a problem, apply an intervention, and
then take repeated ratings of the extent to which the problem has been
ameliorated, reduced, or eliminated (Mutschler, 1979; Randall, 1972). Target problem designs are useful with clients, client systems, and self when
the problem is known and specifiable, but where measurable outcomes are
difficult to specify (Hudson, 1981). The most common data collection
method is a specially designed data collection form (see example below).

The advantages of this method are several. When used in clinical practice, this method of evaluation is fairly nonintrusive and easily accepted by
clients (Martens & Holmstrup, 1974). The activity of eliciting from the client information regarding the problem situation is usually a necessary first
step anyway, and when clients have difficulty formulating problems the use
of this measure can help clarify problems and focus discussion. Furthermore, the simplicity of the instrument makes it useful when working with
clients who are low-functioning or of limited education and verbal ability.
This design is also applicable to administrative practice, where it is often
necessary and efficient to concentrate on the elimination of problems.

The limits of this method are its one-dimensional focus on problems
with little attention to specifying desirable outcomes. You may find that
you have succeeded in resolving a problem, but this will not tell where this
achievement has taken you.

Elements Required

Problem Statement?   Yes. The problem is stated in qualitative or
                      quantitative terms by the client(s) and the
                      practitioner. A researcher using a target problem
                      design usually selects a series of problems and
                      states them in behavioral terms (mother and son
                      argue all the time, daughter has low self-image,
                      etc.).

Goal Statement?   No. The goal is implicit and understood to be the
                      partial or complete alleviation of the stated
                      problems.

Observable Outcomes?   No. The expected outcome is conceptualized as
                          change in the problem. Change is implicitly
                          defined as the difference between the extent of
                          the problem at first and last measurement given a
                          certain degree of severity.

Measurement Tool?   Yes. Two scales are applied independently by the
                          client and by the practitioner and are repeated as
                          many times as desired.
                          Degree of Severity Scale. This is a simple
                          categorical scale consisting of five ratings:

NP	No Problem
NVS	Not Very Severe
S	Severe
VS	Very Severe
ES	Extremely Severe

                          Improvement Scale. This is a simple five-point
                          ordinal scale used at termination (and follow-up if
                          possible):

1	Worse
2	No Change
3	A Little Better
4	Somewhat Better
5	A Lot Better

Intervention   No. This method requires no specification or
Identified?   description of the intervention.

Multipurpose Design?   Yes. This method can be used in process
                         evaluation because the social worker (as client)
                         can select the problems (areas of performance,
                         interaction, etc. needing improvement or skill
                         development) and then evaluate the degree to
                         which this problem in performance has been
                         eliminated. This design can also be used to
                         evaluate the outcomes of practice in clinical or
                         organizational settings.

Reliability and   Strupp and Bloxom (1975) found in clinical
Validity?   settings that the target problem severity ratings
                         were significantly correlated with clients' and
                         clinicians' ratings on other improvement scales
                         and are, therefore, fairly reliable. No measures of
                         validity are available.

Directions for Doing Target Problem Scrutiny

There are five steps in using target problem designs (see following form):

Target Problem and Global Improvement Scale

Target Problem (rated by)	Target Problem Rating (Degree of Severity)			Target Problem Rating (Change Scale)		Global Improvement Rating
	Start	Time1	Time2	Termination	Follow-Up	

1. Identify the number of persons to be included in the evaluation cohort (there can be one or more persons who are the target of the intervention).
2. Each person lists the problem(s) that are to be the focus of the intervention.
3. Each problem is then rated using the degree of severity scale (this becomes the baseline assessment).

4. The degree of severity rating is repeated as many times as desired throughout the period of interest.

5. At the end of the evaluation period the improvement scale is used to assess the amount of change across the repeated measures and as a follow-up measurement.

Sybil was a marriage counselor working with a very difficult couple. It was not readily apparent to her what approach to take, so she designed an outcome assessment to test whether she had made the right decision.

Sybil Johns, ACSW, worked for the Sunnydale Family Counseling Service. She has just been assigned the Wilson family, who came to family counseling at the request of their attorney. They complained of marital discord and stated that they planned to divorce. Counseling was their last-ditch attempt to save their marriage. Sybil usually used confrontational techniques in her counselling, but she had a hunch that confrontation would not be useful with this family. Since her research question was about the Wilsons, she chose a single-system approach.

Sybil nearly always followed the approach of describing two to four specific problems in the marriage, identifying the participants in these problems, and then setting up situations in which these problems could be confronted. In short, confrontation was Sybil's independent variable. She was very confident of her ability to use this technique. She had used it with many families and with good success in the past. She had never before, however, used it with a couple who had already decided that they wanted a divorce. The target of her study, then, was the Wilson family. Since she was interested in what outcome her approach would have on this particular family, her research question was: Will confrontational therapy improve the situation in the Wilson family?

At the intake session, Sybil had a hard time getting the Wilsons to focus on specific problems. Both of them took the position that the marriage was a shambles and that it was the other partner's fault. Sybil felt that she could not proceed with therapy if she could not get the partners to focus on specific problems, and at this point she could not define an outcome to measure because the problems were stated so globally that she had no way to measure any change.

In an attempt to operationalize the dependent variable, at the start of the next session she insisted that each partner write down three specific things that made them angry. The rest of the session was spent clarifying these problem areas. Mrs. Wilson listed three problems: He runs around with other women; he never gives me any money of my own; he never helps take care of the children. Mr. Wilson listed: She runs around with other men; she spends money like it was water; she can't control the kids. The discussion revealed that both Mr. and Mrs. Wilson had been unfaithful, that they had major disagreements as to who was allowed to spend family income and for what purposes (this seemed to be the ground on which power and control issues were fought), and that there were major disagreements as to how children were to be reared and disciplined.

Sybil decided that she would use improvement in these problem areas as an indicator of the effectiveness of her technique with this family. Since these were very large problem areas and she could not define specific measures of progress, she chose to use the target problem approach. She realized that for the most part the only measure she could get was the clients' perception of change in these areas. She listed the three problem areas as she perceived them.

At the next session she had the Wilsons rate each problem as ES for extremely serious, VS for very serious, S for serious, NVS for not very serious, and NP for no problem. Then Sybil rated the problems using the same scale.

This assessment of the Wilsons' marital problems was repeated at 3 months and again at 6 months, when counseling was terminated. At this time they also evaluated the degree to which their marital situation had changed and their overall improvement.

At the point of termination and again at the six month follow-up, Sybil studied the reported change in the problem areas and found that her intervention had led to improvement in all problem areas as perceived by all three observers (Figure 3.4). She was somewhat concerned that Mr. Wilson's assess-

FIGURE 3.4. Wilsons' target problem and global improvement scale.

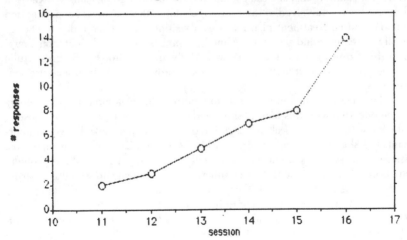

ment of improvement in the marriage was less positive than Mrs. Wilson's. But since the Wilsons agreed to continue with counseling and were again living together, Sybil decided that Mr. Wilson was by nature more critical.

Sybil concluded that confrontation had been an effective technique with the Wilsons, and she resolved to investigate its use with other types of couples. She stored the Wilsons' data so she could aggregate it with information from other cases.

Julie is a rehabilitation social worker assigned to the burn unit of Center City Hospital. She does a single-subject study to monitor the progress of a young girl's in-home treatment plan.

Julie James has been a social worker with the visiting nurse program in Center City for 12 years. Her job is to work with families who are caring for their severely ill children at home. Visiting Nurses has several services that they offer to these families, and they have access to many other services that are available through other community agencies. Julie serves as a case manager, she assesses the family's needs and coordinates the services they receive. She is convinced that all of the services are effective for some families and that all are well-administered.

Julie has recently received a request from Dr. Kidwell of Pediatric Services, Inc. to work with the Carlson family, whose daughter Holly is about to be released from the hospital after 3 months in the severe burn unit. Holly suffered burns over three fourths of her body as a result of an automobile accident. She is severely disfigured and will have to return to the hospital for reconstructive surgery at least four times over the next 3 years. Mrs. Carlson was driving when Holly was injured, and although the other driver was at fault, she still feels guilty about the accident.

While hospital staff have tried to teach Mrs. Carlson to change Holly's dressings and to do rehabilitative exercises with Holly, she has been very resistive, claiming that she can't stand to cause her daughter pain. Mr. Carlson has also been uninvolved in the process, claiming that business keeps him tied up. The initial treatment plan includes a visiting nurse once a day to change Holly's dressings and monitor her medical process and a rehabilitation therapist three times per week to work with Holly and monitor her progress. Julie will go to the home at least once per week to provide psychological adjustment services.

Because Julie had questions as to whether this treatment plan was going to be effective with this family, she decided to monitor this case very closely. She knew that the medical and rehabilitation treatments for Holly were important, but she felt that unless Mr. and Mrs. Carlson dealt with their emotional issues little progress would be made with the child. She saw three problem areas in this case. First, Holly was sullen and withdrawn and would not participate in physical therapy. Further, she had completely stopped talking. Second, Mrs. Carlson was unwilling to help in the treatment process. Third, Mr. Carlson seemed detached and was providing little psychosocial support to either his wife or his daughter. To monitor the case Julie decided to use a target problem approach with herself as the informant. After 2 months of involvement with this family, Julie saw little or no progress toward change in the problem areas (Figure 3.5). Julie's assessment was verified by the nurse and the rehabilitation therapist, both of whom reported little progress. She presented these findings at the next staff meeting and asked for suggestions for further services or a change in approach. One of the other social workers reported that the chaplain at the hospital was starting a support group for parents of severely disabled children and that he would be willing to ask the

FIGURE 3.5. Carlsons' target problem and global improvement scale at 2 months.

Target Problem (rated by) Social Worker	Target Problem Rating (Degree of Severity)			Target Problem Rating (Change Scale)		Global Rating
	Start	1 MO.	2 MO.	Termination	Follow-Up	
Holly's withdrawal	*ES*	*ES*	*ES*			
Mother's refusal to be involved in treatment	*VS*	*VS*	*VS*			
Father's detachment	*ES*	*ES*	*ES*			

chaplain to approach the Carlsons about joining the group. Since the chaplain had worked with the family while Holly was in the hospital it was decided that this should be tried. The team also decided that a visiting homemaker should be provided to care for Holly two mornings per week to allow Mrs. Carlson time out for herself. Julie's assessment of this family's problems improved somewhat by the sixth month (Figure 3.6). Based on these data she concluded

FIGURE 3.6. Carlsons' target problem and global improvement scale at 6 months.

Target Problem (rated by) Social Worker	Target Problem Rating (Degree of Severity)			Target Problem Rating (Change Scale)		Global Rating
	4 MO.	5 MO.	6 MO.	Termination	Follow-Up	
Holly's withdrawal	*VS*	*S*	*S*			
Mother's refusal to be involved in treatment	*ES*	*VS*	*E*			
Father's detachment	*ES*	*ES*	*VS*			

that medical rehabilitation alone was not enough for this family and that further efforts would be needed if Mr. Carlson was to take a more active role in Holly's rehabilitation.

At the staff meeting in the 7th month, Julie showed her target problem scale to the visiting nurse, the homemaker, and the physical therapist. They were all concerned about the lack of improvement in Holly's level of communication and agreed that she was interpreting her father's detachment as rejec-

tion. Very carefully they convinced Mr. Carlson that his involvement was crucial to Holly's eventual recovery, and they monitored the case until it was
finally closed. The team was successful, and by the 12th month Holly's withdrawal had ended and her father and mother were able to nurture her through
the remaining medical treatment (Figure 3.7).

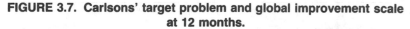

**FIGURE 3.7. Carlsons' target problem and global improvement scale
at 12 months.**

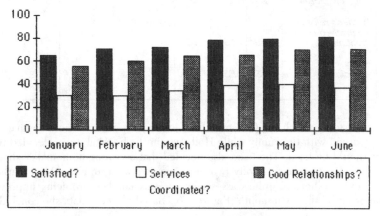

*Jim is a community organizer working for an inner-city
development corporation. He uses target problem scaling to do a
process assessment of his own skill in empowering his clients.*

Jim Jackson works for the Inner City Elderly Services Corporation, an agency
funded by United Way and the Area Agency on Aging. His mission is to teach
organizing skills to elderly residents of the inner city; to empower them to act
on their own behalf in seeking improved city services. He feels he has had
limited success.

The agency serves the two census tracts with the highest crime rates in
the county. Because many of the problems bringing the elderly to the agency
were related to the stress and anxiety of living with the threat of crime as well
as loss to actual theft, crime protection became the central focusing theme of
Jim's organizing efforts. He began a neighborhood association of elderly residents, the goal of which was to pressure police agencies for better protection
and to advocate for the creation of a neighborhood watch program. His effort
to organize the program went very well at the beginning, but after 6 months
its accomplishments have leveled off with little more forward movement. He
knows that as the initial energy of the group flagged, he became too insistent,
trying to push participants into action rather than being patient and teaching
by example rather than by directive. In essence, he was over-involved; he was
doing the work rather than developing the organization to do the work.

Jim knew he must do something. He decided to do an assessment of the
problem with himself as the target of the study. Because the focus of his atten-

tion was this problem and its alleviation, he elected to use a target problem scaling design. He could have specified an outcome measure, such as the creation and maintenance of the neighborhood watch program, but its outcomes would be too long in coming. A process evaluation limited to an examination of the problem would be more immediate and helpful.

Jim's supervisor agreed to participate in the assessment and give Jim help in changing his intervention style. To monitor these changes they developed a target problem improvement scale (Figure 3.8). Jim and his director decided to make four measurements during the 6-month period.

FIGURE 3.8. Jim's target problem and global improvement scale of a neighborhood intervention.

Target Problem (rated by)	TARGET PROBLEM RATING						Global Improve-ment
		Degree of Severity			Degree of Change		
	Start	Time1	Time2	Time3	End	Followup	
Jim:							
doesn't allow elderly to speak for the group	S	S	NVS	NP	5	5	
wants to be in charge of decisions	VS	VS	S	S	3	3	
encourages clients to be dependent	VS	S	S	NVS	4	4	
isn't modeling self advocacy	ES	S	NP	NP	4	5	4
Director:							
Jim is meeting his needs, not the group's needs	VS	S	NVS	NVS	4	4	
Jim wants to "do" rather than model	VS	S	NVS	NP	4	5	
Jim lacks patients	ES	VS	VS	NVS	3	5	5

Severity Scale
NP = No Problem
NVS = Not Very Severe
S = Severe
VS = Very Severe
ES = Extremely Severe

Improvement Scale
1 = Worse
2 = No Change
3 = A Little Better
4 = Somewhat Better
5 = A Lot Better

When the self-assessment was completed, Jim realized that it had become an intervention in and of itself. The introspection he forced on himself in the course of monitoring his own behavior had become the catalyst for his behavior change. As his interaction with the elderly residents improved, so too did the program. There was ample group energy available to get the neighborhood watch project implemented.

Maggie is a human services planner with a community problem involving foster care agencies that is threatening to disrupt service. After implementing her solution, Maggie conducts a survey of the agencies to determine its effectiveness.

Maggie works in the Human Services Division of the Regional Planning Agency. She has responsibility for a wide range of service sectors, including child welfare services. Her agency has just accepted a contract from the United Way for technical assistance aimed at solving a systemic problem.

Over the past few years the relationship between the Department of Human Services (DHS), the child welfare agencies with foster care programs, and the police departments (there are 19 in the affected counties) has been deteriorating. The bickering grew to crisis proportions when last week the police arrested two DHS workers for child neglect and endangerment. The charges were based on an incident involving a child victim of physical abuse who was left sitting in a police department waiting room for an 8-hour period at night. The controversy has involved all agencies in the foster care system and has degenerated into accusations and finger pointing.

In fashioning a solution Maggie first did an informal survey of the police departments and child welfare agencies to determine what they believed was the source of the problem. She got an almost unanimous response: "Not enough emergency foster care slots!" Maggie had reason, however, to doubt this assessment. Hesitant to implement a solution (developing more foster care slots) based on a faulty assessment of the problem, Maggie decided to undertake a short-term planning process. In addition to confirming her hunch about an effective solution, she believed the planning process would itself improve the relationship between the major actors in the foster care program.

A 6-month planning project involved directors and staff from DHS and five child care agencies, the six largest police departments, and the United Way. In the beginning hostility among the agency directors was so intense that Maggie felt she was doing group therapy. She focused the group on exchanging information about themselves—the services they provide and their eligibility criteria. As this process took hold, it became clear that these administrators had very little knowledge about each other. For example, they did not understand that each of the foster care programs was mandated to serve a specific subpopulation and was prohibited from placing children outside these definitions. There was much confusion about which agency was responsible for what kind of child. It turned out there were five programs serving five different types of children: all children under age 13; abuse victims age 13 to 18; status offenders age 13 to 16; juvenile offenders age 10 to 13; and runaways age 12 to 18.

As the lack of information and misinformation was reduced, the real source of the problem became clear to everyone—and it wasn't a lack of after-hour slots, it was misinformation. When a police officer picked up a child at night he usually called an on-call worker at random from one of the six agencies. Because of past confusion about program definitions, the officer had no confidence that the worker he first called would respond, so he would usually call all the on-call workers, hoping to get one to respond. The workers, knowing that the police were calling everyone, would stay in bed hoping that another worker would respond. When no one responded, the police assumed there were no slots available or that the workers were derelict in their duty.

The solution, once it surfaced, was straightforward and easy to implement. Maggie prepared an interagency agreement that specified what category of child each agency was responsible for during after hours. According to the agreement, the agencies promised to respond within 30 minutes if the police officer could tell them that the child fell within their mandated service population. If, however, the child was what was called a "grey area" child (the officer could not categorize the child), then the agencies agreed on a rotation system. For a month at a time, each agency would take its turn placing grey area kids for one night in return for a promise from the other agencies of a staff meeting before noon the following day to make permanent arrangements.

The formal agreement was signed at a much-publicized press conference, after which all police personnel were trained in its use. Posters were printed for all departments outlining the procedure to be followed and were posted by all police phones.

Maggie was very interested in making sure that the interagency agreement was indeed the answer to the problem. She therefore designed an outcome study targeted at the perceptions of all the agencies involved in the system. She wanted to know whether this intervention had the effect of reducing the level of hostility and confusion and changing perceptions about the number of available slots. She collected data via a survey (Figure 3.9) that was

FIGURE 3.9 Maggie's foster care survey form.

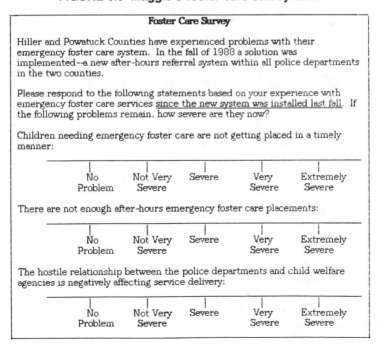

distributed three times: just prior to the implementation of the new system and 6 and 12 months after the implementation.

When the data were collected she aggregated them using a target problem improvement scale; that is, she averaged the responses from the three different types of organizations so that she could compare the results. As can be seen from her scale (Figure 3.10), perception about the problem and its

FIGURE 3.10. Maggie's target problem scale for community problem.

Target Problem (rated by)	TARGET PROBLEM RATING Degree of Severity			GLOBAL IMPROVEMENT Degree of Change
	Prior	6 mos.	12 mos.	
Police Departments:				
• Children needing emergency foster care are not getting placed in a timely manner.	ES	S	NVS	
• There are not enough after-hours emergency foster care placements	ES	NVS	NP	
• The hostility between police and child welfare agencies is negatively affecting the service delivery system.	ES	VS	S	4
Depart. of Human Services:				
• Children needing emergency foster care are not getting placed in a timely manner.	ES	S	NVS	
• There are not enough after-hours emergency foster care placements	ES	VS	NVS	
• The hostility between police and child welfare agencies is negatively affecting the service delivery system.	ES	ES	NVS	5
Child Welfare Agencies:				
• Children needing emergency foster care are not getting placed in a timely manner.	VS	S	NVS	
• There are not enough after-hours emergency foster care placements	ES	NP	NP	
• The hostility between police and child welfare agencies is negatively affecting the service delivery system.	ES	ES	NVS	5

severity were changed dramatically. All respondents had felt prior to the intervention that these were extremely severe problems, but all rated them no problem or not very severe by the end of the observation period. This scale (Figure 3.10) became the nucleus of her final report to the director of the United Way, who was very pleased with the outcome of their contract.

GOAL ATTAINMENT SCALING

Whereas target problem designs focus on the problem statement and use it as a measurement of outcome, goal attainment scaling (GAS) designs use the goal statement as the criteria for evaluation (Mager, 1972). Goal attainment designs are appropriate when an appraisal outcome—the condition or behavior being sought by the intervention—is more important than an appraisal of the problematic state, situation, or behavior. Like target problem scaling, this design uses an individualized instrument for recording the data (Kiresuk & Garwick, 1979; Kiresuk & Lund, 1977).

Although goal attainment scaling is included in this chapter on qualitative designs, it can take a qualitative or a quantitative approach to self-assessment. This is a particularly useful method given the current emphasis on quality assurance. In medical settings and family services, for example, social services must often set quality assurance standards and then meet them (Rock, 1987). Goal attainment scaling is an individualized approach to assessment that is capable of producing a quantitative assessment of outcomes measured against a standard stated in either qualitative or quantitative terms. Further, this method can also be used by practitioners to focus on themselves via goals having to do with skill or personal development.

The advantages of goal attainment scaling start with its flexibility. It is probably the most versatile method described in this guide. It is easily adapted to any level of practice, any field, and process or outcome evaluation. Its other advantages are that its implementation requires no modification of the intervention, its degree of face validity is seldom in question, and the data derived from its use with single subjects/systems can easily be aggregated.

The limitations are those inherent in all evaluations based on outcomes. First, seldom can outcomes be attributed directly to the intervention because of multiple confounding factors found in both the process itself and in the environment and culture of the client/client system. Second, it is sometimes difficult to use an assessment method that relies on outcome statements because they may be either very difficult to make explicit or be very long in coming. Last, there are situations in which an outcome-based evaluation is undesirable because it requires you to select the expectations of an outcome and then restrict them to a relevant, realistic, and measurable indicator.

Elements Required

Problem Statement?   No. There need be no explicit, detailed description of the problem. There is, of course, recognition that a problem, situation, or state of affairs exists that requires attention, but little or no effort must be spent to understand its full dimensionality.

Goal Statement?

Yes. This method requires the systematic identification, specification, and operationalization of goals in measurable terms. These statements are then used as measures of outcomes.

Observable
Outcomes?

No. The expected outcome is conceptualized as a change in the extent to which the client/client system has reached the goal. Change is explicitly defined as the difference between the degree to which the goal is achieved at intake and the extent to which the goal has been reached at termination of the intervention.

Measurement Tool?

Yes. Each goal is scaled individually for the client/client system using a five-point scale that ranges from much less than expected change to much more than expected change.

Intervention Method?

No. This method requires no specification or description of the intervention method.

Multipurpose Design?

Yes. This method can easily be adapted to clinical, organizational, or community settings. All it requires is a little imagination and creativity in writing goals and then in scaling them. For this reason, it has great potential for macro practice where intervention is complex, multidimensional, and elusive, but where broad goals can be specified.

Reliability and
Validity?

Studies have shown that reliability of goal attainment instruments ranges from adequate to good (Rock, 1987). There is disagreement, however, regarding validity. Studies of concurrent validity obtained poor correlation between GAS scores and standardized tests (Seaberg & Gillespie, 1975). Rock (1987) states that there is validity to the idea that goals in the helping process that already are established as vitally important to that process will be focused upon, clarified, and moderately well measured by following the procedures of GAS.

Directions for Doing Goal Attainment Scaling

There are six steps in using Goal Attainment Scaling (see form below):

Goal Attainment Scale

Levels of Predicted Attainment	Scale #1 Specify: Wt.	Scale #2 Specify: Wt.	Scale #3 Specify: Wt.
Much Less than the expected level of outcome (-2)			
Somewhat less than the expected level of outcome (-1)			
Expected level of outcome (0)			
Somewhat more than the expected level of outcome (+1)			
Much more than the expected level of outcome (+2)			

* **Baseline**   ** **Termination**

1. Identify the goal(s) for the client/client system. Single or multiple goals can be selected by an expert, committee, practitioner, client, or a combination of all these persons. Each goal must be a concise statement of a desired outcome (an end, a future state), not a statement of the method needed to achieve the end.

2. The goal(s) must then be scaled. Each goal is measured on a five-point scale ranging from -2 to $+2$:

    -2 much less than expected level of outcome

    -1 somewhat less than expected level of outcome

    0 expected level of outcome

    $+1$ somewhat more than expected level of outcome

    $+2$ much more than expected level of outcome.

    For each of these five points, the expected outcomes must be made operational by statements that indicate the referents for the degree of attaining the goal. The referents may be behavioral, indicators of emotional states, or indicators of group or community activity.

3. Each scale is then assigned a weight (ranging from 1 to 10) indicating the importance of each goal in the overall intervention plan.

4. At the beginning of the intervention, the point on the scale at which the client/client system should be rated for each goal is determined (this is the baseline measure).

5. Repeated measures are taken during intervention, at termination, and during follow-up if possible.

6. A composite outcome score—the GAS score—is then computed as follows:

    a. The Gain/Loss Score is computed for each scale by taking the difference between the baseline and last measurement (if there is a gain, then the sign is a plus; if a loss, then the sign is a minus).

    b. Each Gain/Loss Score is multiplied by its weight.

    c. The resulting products are summed to obtain the composite GAS score.

Betty is a social worker learning to use art therapy as a tool of crime investigation. She uses goal attainment scaling to monitor and improve her skill.

Betty Green has recently completed her M.S.W. in forensic social work and has been hired by the Bay City Police Department to work in their victim assistance program. She is a sworn police officer and her job is to help victims deal emotionally with what has happened to them and to obtain information that will help in the arrest and conviction of the perpetrator. Betty tries to obtain the necessary information in ways that will minimize the emotional harm to the victim.

Recently Betty has been assigned to a case in which a three-year-old boy was killed on a playground. The only known witness is a three-year-old girl who was on the playground with the victim at the time of the crime. Her name is Connie Johnson, she is minimally verbal, and she is clearly traumatized by what she has witnessed. Her parents have given permission for Betty to work with Connie to obtain whatever information she can. At the outset, all Betty knows is that the two children were together and Connie was the one who summoned help by running to a neighbor's crying that a man had hurt Billy. Connie was in no way physically harmed in the attack. The officer who initially investigated the crime reported talking with Connie, and he is convinced that she saw the crime occur and that she does not know the perpetrator.

Betty practices art therapy as a technique for helping children work through traumatic material. She often uses art as a nonthreatening means of enabling children to express painful or shocking information that they cannot talk about. The basic process is to encourage children to draw pictures that represent an event and how they feel about the event, and then invite them to tell what is going on in the picture.

Because she has never used this technique with a child this young, Betty wants to be very careful that she does nothing to further harm Connie. She set three goals for herself to monitor whether she is using the technique properly:

1. *I will use art therapy in such a way that Connie does not suffer unnecessarily*. Betty gave this goal a weight of seven because she felt that it was crucial that she do nothing that would increase Connie's trauma.
2. *I will end every session on a positive note*. Betty operationalized this goal by wrapping up each session with a hug and by reassuring Connie that she is doing well. She gave this goal a weight of 5.
3. *I will never pressure Connie to proceed into material that she seems unwilling or unable to deal with*. Betty gave this goal a weight of 10 because she understood that the technique is maximally effective when the child feels safe and unpressured.

Betty developed a goal attainment scale to operationalize these goals (Figure 3.11) so that she could use them to monitor and guide her throughout the therapy. She then decided that this case offered real opportunity for new learning, so she engaged an experienced play therapist to observe the sessions with Connie and to judge her performance against the goals she had established.

During the first session, Connie drew a knife hidden behind a bush. Betty began asking her who put the knife there, where the bush was, and if it had something to do with Billy. This caused Connie to withdraw and tear up the picture. Betty ended the session with a hug but was very disappointed with the first session. Betty's consultant scored the first scale with a −2 because he felt she had increased Connie's trauma; he scored the second scale with a 0 because Betty had hugged her and thanked her and to some extent ended the session positively; he scored the third scale with a −2 because

FIGURE 3.11. Betty's goal attainment scale for intervention with Connie.

Levels of Predicted Attainment	Scale #1 Connie does not suffer Needlessly Wt. 7	Scale #2 Betty ends each session in a positive manner Wt. 5	Scale #3 Betty does not put pressure on Connie Wt. 10
Much Less Than Expected Level of Outcome (-2)	*I increase the trauma Connie is suffering*	*I fail to hug Connie and thank her*	*I get too involved in seeking evidence and push Connie to talk about things she is not ready for*
Somewhat less than Expected Level of Outcome (-1)	*Connie continues having nightmares*	*I hug her but don't really communicate my caring*	*I probe rather than let Connie set the pace*
Expected Level of Outcome (0)	*Connie is able to verbalize about the murder without being traumatized*	*I hug her and let her know that I like and appreciate her*	*I let Connie set the pace guided by my questions*
Somewhat More Than Expected Level of Outcome (+1)	*Connie is no longer afraid to go outside*	*I find a way to communicate real caring and concern to Connie*	*I am able to relax and let Connie deal with the situation at her own pace*
Much More Than Expected Level of Outcome (+2)	*Connie is no longer fearful and regains her confidence*	*I develop a strong rapport with Connie*	*I let Connie pace the sessions and do not press for information*

Betty had really pushed Connie hoping to solve the case quickly. The composite weighted score was $-2 \times 7 = -14$, $0 \times 5 = 0$, $-2 \times 10 = -20$ for a total of -34. Betty agreed that she had not done well in this first session.

With new resolve, Betty went into the second session the next day determined to let Connie tell the story in her own way. Betty began the session by inviting Connie to play with some dolls; Betty then asked Connie if she would draw pictures of the bad dreams she had been having. Connie again drew the knife in the bush, but this time Betty did not mention the knife. Instead, she asked Connie to draw some more and to tell what the picture was about. At the end of this session, the consultant gave Betty zeros on all scales. By combining the observations of a neutral person that were structured by herself, Betty was able to use the intervention as a learning situation and successfully engage herself in self-improvement. She did not get the information that she needed in session two, but with patience it did surface by session four.

> Ron is the intake worker for a residential treatment facility for delinquent youths. He examines his decision-making ability by means of an outcome study.

Ron Bennet has worked at the Smooth Sailing School, a residential program for delinquent children, for the 6 years since he obtained his B.A. in social work. The school's program is based on a positive peer culture model. Ron has been a child care worker and a counselor and is now the intake worker. As the intake worker, it is Ron's responsibility to review all of the information available on referrals, interview the child and her/his parents, and make a decision regarding the probability that the program will be successful. While Smooth Sailing has not experienced major budget cuts, they have had to be more careful with their resources. The director has told Ron that it is important that they tighten up their admission procedure because they cannot afford to use space for children who are not going to be successful in their program.

Ron has decided that a good indicator of his effectiveness at intake is the extent of progress that each child has shown by the time of the 3-month staff meeting. This staff meeting is attended by the child's parent(s), the worker from the referring agency, the probation officer if there is one, a representative of the school, and the supervisor of the cottage where the child resides. At this conference, the child's progress is reviewed, a decision is made about continued placement and the treatment plan is reassessed. Ron believes that those children who are going to be successful in the Smooth Sailing program will begin to show signs of change by the time of the 3-month review.

To test his ability to make good intake decisions, Ron decided to set three specific goals for each child he admits and to ask the cottage director and the school teacher to rate the child's progress on these goals at the 3-month review. Ron selected the goal attainment scaling approach because it is self-anchoring; that is, the goals and levels of attainment can be established for each specific child. He decided that he would set the goals and levels at the time of intake but let others make the judgment as to the levels of achievement. In this way, Ron avoided any subjective bias on his part by having others do the actual rating.

Roger Wilder, age 16, was referred to Smooth Sailing by the juvenile court of Slattery County. He had been in various kinds of trouble for the last 3 years, and if he had not been accepted by Smooth Sailing he would have been sent to Hardrock State School for Delinquents. Roger came from a middle-class family, his two older siblings had not been in major trouble, and the family was intact. The records revealed that Roger was at least 2 years behind grade level in every subject except math, where he was about 2 years ahead. He was a computer hacker and, in fact, his most recent problem with the law had to do with gaining access to a local bank's computer and altering some of their records. Roger often had violent temper outbursts and had been disruptive in the classroom. His teacher reported that Roger had a very short attention span and often tried to involve other children in his disruptive behaviors. She called him very verbal and a negative leader.

Ron admitted Roger to the program and set the following goals:

1. Roger will make progress toward performing at grade level. This goal he weighted a 7 because he felt that poor academic performance was the root of many of Roger's problems.

2. Roger will learn appropriate ways to express anger. This he weighted a 3 because he felt that this would be solved as Roger began to develop positive behaviors.
3. Roger will learn to be a positive rather than a negative leader. Ron weighted this third goal a 9 because he felt that since Roger was a leader, it was important that he learn to use these skills in positive ways.

Ron wrote a goal attainment rating scale for Roger (Figure 3.12). At the 3-month conference the school principal gave the following ratings; progress

FIGURE 3.12. Ron's goal attainment scale.

Levels of Predicted Attainment	Scale #1 Roger achieves appropriate grade level Wt. 7	Scale #2 Roger expresses anger appropriately Wt. e	Scale #3 Roger displays positive leadership Wt.
Much Less Than Expected Level of Outcome (−2)	*falls behind current level*	*acts out in more destructive ways*	*uses others all the time to achieve negative goals*
Somewhat Less than Expected Level of Outcome (−1)	*stays at current level*	*stays the same*	*sometimes uses others to achieve negative goals*
Expected Level of Outcome (0)	*gains three months*	*shows some signs expressing anger in acceptable ways*	*sometimes functions as a positive leader*
Somewhat More Than Expected Level of Outcome (+1)	*gains six months*	*rarely has tantrums*	*has become a strong but inconsistent leader*
Much More Than Expected Level of Outcome (+2)	*gains a year*	*always expresses anger in acceptable ways*	*never functions as a negative leader*

toward grade level = 1; appropriate anger expression = 0; positive leadership = −1. Ron computed a composite weighted score of −2. The cottage director gave the following ratings: progress toward grade level = 1; appropriate anger expression = −1; positive leadership = 1, for a weighted composite score of 5. The average of the two raters was 1.5. Based upon these ratings Ron concluded that Roger was a borderline but valid admission to the program.

The director of Smooth Sailing liked the scale when Ron shared it with him, and they began using the scales every 3 months to monitor their effectiveness with each child. Ron also began aggregating the information across children and learned that an average between the two raters of 5 or higher at 3 months indicated a high likelihood of success and, therefore, that he had done a good job at intake.

Cecil is director of a family service agency experiencing changes that are affecting Cecil's administrative effectiveness. She elects to do a process assessment with herself as target.

Cecil Cooper is the director of FAMILY, a large private family service agency that provides a broad range of clinical, case management, and advocacy services to families and children. She has been director for 5 years—very difficult years during which the technologies of psychosocial treatment and child welfare services have increased in complexity while resources have dwindled. The squeeze has been intense; Expectations of clients and staff in regard to the effectiveness of service outcomes have risen dramatically, while at the same time Cecil has been forced to decrease unit costs.

Cecil has just returned from a long-overdue, badly needed vacation. Sitting on the beach she had the luxury of reflecting on the state of her agency and, most importantly, on her own performance as its leader. She has come back to work having reached two conclusions. First, she is sure her organization will have to downsize over the next few years and that she must begin to prepare herself and the agency for this eventuality. Second, she is concerned that, as a result of the current stress of managing FAMILY, she is being sucked into a management style inimical to her philosophy of leadership. Although she believes in a participative style of management, she realizes she has been making most of the difficult decisions herself. She now believes this is at least partially responsible for the strained relationship between herself and much of the supervisory staff.

Cecil plans a project designed to take action on both of these concerns at the same time. She initiates an internal planning process involving the entire organization, the purpose of which is the development of a 5-year strategic plan. She hopes that as the staff gains an understanding of the problems facing the organization, they will become more accepting of the changes that are coming. She also intends to make a conscious effort to return to a more democratic style of management. To test her ability to succeed in this regard, she designs a self-assessment process.

Since Cecil can be explicit about her goal, she elects to do goal attainment scaling. She decides to adopt an 8-month time frame for the planning process and to survey the staff at two points in the process for their perceptions of the degree to which she is conducting the project in a democratic way. She designs the goal attainment scale (Figure 3.13). Cecil decides that each goal is equally important, so she does not give them weights. She then designs a survey form (Figure 3.14) that is short and to the point.

When the project had concluded after 8 months, Cecil took time out to

FIGURE 3.13. Cecil Cooper's goal attainment scale for developing a democratic leadership style.

Levels of Predicted Attainment	Scale #1 Specify: I conduct the strategic planning process in a participative style, encouraging maximum involvement from the maximum number of staff *	Scale #2 Specify: I manage decision making so that all staff have input and participate in reaching consensus about strategic plans. *
Much Less than the expected level of outcome (-2)	I involve no one but myself and the staff invests no effort in the strategic planning process. **	I make all the decisions and announce them to the staff and directors. **
Somewhat less than the expected level of outcome (-1)	I involve some of the staff but allow them no opportunity to take responsibility for the process.	I make all the decision and then "sell" them to the staff
Expected level of outcome. (0)	I involve some of the staff and allow them to manage the process, but only until things get crucial-- then I take over.	I present the problems, get suggestions from the staff, and make the decisions. ***
Somewhat more than the expected level of outcome (+1)	I involve most of the staff and allow them to manage the process under my supervision. ***	I define the question and the parameters of the solutions, then ask the staff to make the decision.
Much more than the expected level of outcome. (+2)	I involve all of the staff and encourage them to manage the process within the limits that we discuss and agree upon.	I make it possible for the staff to reach consensus on strategic decisions concerning the future of our organization.

* Baseline   ** Time Two   ***Time Three

tabulate the results of her self-assessment and to think about the future. She tabulated the results of the goal attainment scaling (Table 3.1).

Cecil felt good about the results (the GAS score was 3.5) and realized that the act of focusing on her own practice for a time had been very instrumental in helping her to change her behavior. The plan that had been adopted would be difficult to implement, but would have been impossible without the process that had accompanied its development.

FIGURE 3.14. Cecil's feedback survey.

To:	All Staff
From:	Cecil

In an effort to improve my management skills I am doing a self-assessment and need your help. Please answer these two questions honestly and candidly. Mark your answer on the five point scale and put the form in the box on the counter in the lunchroom. Please do not put your name on the form. Thank you for your cooperation.

1. To what extent do I conduct the business of this agency in a participative style, encouraging maximum involvement from the maximum number of staff?

-2	-1	0	+1	+2
No Extent		Some Extent		Maximum Extent

2. To what extent do I manage decision making so that all staff have input and participate in reaching consensus about our future?

-2	-1	0	+1	+2
No Extent		Some Extent		Maximum Extent

Tony is a social worker for the Department of Special Educational Services of a large regional school district. He has developed a new functional role—Transition Specialist—and decides after three years to do an assessment of his effectiveness.

Highland Greene School District's Department of Special Educational Services (SES) serves 6 high schools and 15 junior highs. This is a multidisciplinary agency offering a wide range of services to behaviorally disordered (BD) and learning-disabled (LD) youngsters as well as other special populations of students with physical and emotional handicaps. Tony had worked at SES for 10 years when he was asked if he would like to develop a new program that would aid BD kids in their transition from high school into adult life.

Tony took the new position as Transition Specialist because he knew there was a very serious problem with BD students once they graduated from high school. There was no governmental agency or local support system to help them find a niche; they often fell through the cracks of existing programs.

TABLE 3.1. Results of Cecil's Self-Assessment project

	Issue #1	Issue #2
Baseline	.2	1.7
Conclusion	1.3	4.1
Gain/Loss Score	1.1	2.4

Shortly after becoming Transition Specialist, Tony was able to determine that numerous agencies were potential resources for BD students, but none had direct responsibility for them:

> *Vocational Rehabilitation*—the state agency providing screening, diagnosis, job readiness, job training, and job coaching to persons having physical handicaps or mental illnesses (that meet the DSM-III-R criteria).
>
> *Comprehensive Community Mental Health Center*—a local agency providing in- and outpatient mental health treatment to persons with a wide range of emotional problems, including those with chronic mental illnesses.
>
> *Department of Human Services*—the state agency that administers Social Security Supplemental Income to persons with chronic disabilities.
>
> *Skills, Inc.*—a community agency providing job training and shelter workshop services to persons with developmental disabilities and chronic mental illnesses.
>
> *Juvenile Court*—part of the state judicial system that is able to provide some limited programs through probation services to the behaviorally disordered youngsters that get caught up in the juvenile justice system (which many do).

The first few cases that Tony accepted for transition services taught him an important lesson: No matter how well he did his job on behalf of a client, his effort would be totally ineffectual if the other needed agencies were unwilling to provide services.

One case served as an unfortunate example of the problem Tony encountered. Jeff had been a student in Highland Greene's BD classes throughout high school. He had been in juvenile court several times and had been in foster care at least twice because of a very unstable family life. In spite of these deficits, Jeff had stayed in school and the SES team believed he could make it on his own after leaving school—if he had some help. Tony quickly learned that putting help to work for Jeff was very difficult. In order for him to receive vocational rehabilitation services, Tony was told that Jeff would have to be labeled diagnostically eligible by the Mental Health Center. The Mental Health Center staff psychologist who Tony talked with said that according to their records Jeff had been labeled as having an Attention Deficit Disorder (ADD), and she saw no evidence that the question of diagnosis should be reconsidered. Tony then found out that the ADD diagnosis would not entitle Jeff to services from Voc Rehab, Skills, or SSI. Going back to the Mental Health Center, the psychologist refused again to do any further testing, even after Tony told her that SES felt Jeff would benefit greatly from Voc Rehab services. After spending the entire fall semester trying to work around these obstacles, Tony felt he was at a dead end. He felt very discouraged because without these services Jeff's life would be profoundly different from what it could be.

As a last-ditch effort during the spring before Jeff's graduation, Tony convened a staff meeting of those teachers and special education staff who had been involved with Jeff. He also included Jeff's probation worker from Juvenile Court Services and Jeff himself, who had just turned 18. This staff meeting revealed several facts that Tony realized were highly important:

1. The probation worker insisted that the Mental Health Center had never assigned the ADD diagnosis to Jeff. She said it was a possibility at one time, but it had never been confirmed and her office had a complete paper record going back 6 years to prove it. (This meant that either the psychologist hadn't read the record, had read the record but it was incomplete or misleading, or had read the record and didn't want to accept the referral for some reason.)
2. The head of SES special services said that Voc Rehab had the latitude under a "special needs" category to accept Jeff for services and, furthermore, that this acceptance would measurably improve his chances of getting SSI. (This meant that the Voc Rehab staff that Tony had talked with were either unwilling or unable to share their eligibility criteria.)

This experience and others like it led Tony to a very important conclusion: *Unless these agencies had a structure with which to work together on behalf of individual clients, and unless they were willing and able to participate honestly and wholeheartedly, he could not be effective in helping these young people.*

As a result, Tony developed a cooperative project with funding from a local foundation. The 2-year demonstration grant supported a full-time case manager and purchased staff time for interagency staffings from the six participating organizations. In addition, Tony used the teams as a forum to establish working relationships between the agencies regarding the sharing of information. The agencies agreed on procedures protecting confidentiality, privacy, and release of information. They established protocols for multidisciplinary diagnosis and case planning, and backed them up with commitments for services.

Tony must now provide a progress report to the foundation in order to receive continuation funding. In some respects assessing the effectiveness of this project is difficult. If the goal of the project is stated as one of primary prevention ("preventing the wasting of a young life"), measuring something that has been prevented is a real problem. If, on the other hand, it is stated as a treatment goal (enabling youngsters to become productive citizens), the measurement of outcomes might have to wait for years. One way around this conundrum is to reduce the major goal to process-oriented subgoals and to develop from them a measurement scale. Tony decided that, in order to achieve the major goal, there has to be a network of agencies: (1) willing to share accurate and timely information with each other and (2) capable of being responsive to requests for service. Combining these two subgoals with an overall evaluation measure, Tony created a goal attainment scale (Figure 3.15).

Tony distributed this scale to all the members of the interagency teams as

FIGURE 3.15. Tony's goal attainment scale on agency networking effectiveness.

Levels of Predicted Attainment	Scale #1 Within the rules of confidentiality, agencies share information willingly and honestly.	Scale #2 When there is agreement that a client can benefit from transition service, agencies are responsive to referrals.	Scale #3 Overall Evaluation
Much Less than the expected level of outcome (-2)	Agencies actively inhibit the flow of information *	Agencies do not respond unless bullied, shamed, or threatened. *	Things are worse level two years ago. *
Somewhat less than the expected level of outcome (-1)	Agencies provide information, but only after repeated requests.	Agencies do respond, but reluctantly and at their own pace.	Things are somewhat improved.
Expected level of outcome. (0)	Agencies provide the information that is requested	Agencies do respond, but within the perceived limits of their resources.	Things are definitely improved
Somewhat more than the expected level of outcome (+1)	Agencies provide the information requested in a comprehensive and useful manner.	Agencies respond readily, and are willing to stretch their resources if necessary. **	Things are greatly improved
Much more than the expected level of outcome. (+2)	Information is provided in the most comprehensive and useful manner. **	Agencies respond eagerly, and will search for additional resources if necessary.	It's a whole new world! **

* beginning   ** end of two years

well as administrators and supervisors of the participating agencies. He asked them to indicate the level where they thought they were at the beginning of the project and where they were at the end of the 2 years. The overall GAS score was 1.75, a substantial indicator of success and good enough to convince the foundation to provide continuation funding.

4 Quantitative Designs

The 12 self-assessments included in this chapter are quantitative designs—monitoring, baseline, and multiple baselines. Like those in Chapter 3, they are drawn from diverse practices and represent interventions at different levels, but they are used to collect quantitative rather than qualitative data. For a full understanding of these 12 self-assessments, study the section on analysis of numeric data in Chapter 5.

MONITORING DESIGNS

A monitoring design is usually a quantitative method of evaluation. It requires that the behavior(s) or event(s) of interest be measured at several points in time. This design is most useful when clear behavioral indicators of the problem or situation can be specified and measured (Behling & Merves, 1984). It can be used to assess your own behavior as you interact with the client/client system during the process of intervention, or it can be used to monitor the behavior(s) or event(s) that the intervention is intended to bring about (Witkin & Harrison, 1979).

This is not an experimental design, as is the baseline design discussed below. It does not require a baseline period during which the behavior of interest is measured as a control against which change during the intervention can be compared. Without baseline measurement, cause-and-effect claims cannot be made. It is possible, however, to measure change as it occurs over time, and sometimes that is all that is needed.

The advantages of this design are that it provides clear quantitative indicators of change over the course of an intervention. It tends to encourage clear problem definition, and it keeps the helping process focused on the problems identified as requiring intervention. Because there are repeated measures over time, there are statistics that can give you valid indexes of change.

The disadvantage of this design is that it requires defining one or more clear behavioral referents. Referents, once specified and focused upon, may be reactive and change the problem simply by becoming the focus. This design, because of the need for repeated measures, can also be fairly intrusive, depending on the behavior selected for measurement and the means selected for monitoring it.

Elements Required

Problem Statement?	Yes. The problem or situation of interest must be stated before the behavioral referents can be selected.
Goal Statement?	Yes. This method requires specification of the direction and level of change to be achieved by termination. It does not require, however, detailed and scaled goal statements as in GAS.
Observable Outcomes?	Yes. To use this method you must specify the expected outcomes and the observable measure of those outcomes.
Measurement Tool?	Yes. The problem of interest and the behavior indicators that have been selected define what is to be measured. You must specify how the measurement will be recorded.
Intervention Method?	No. While you may specify specific interventions, it is not a requirement of the design. You can monitor changes in behaviors or events regardless of what type of methods are being used.
Multipurpose Design?	Yes. You can use this design to monitor clinical processes by measuring your behavior or the client/client system's behavior.
Reliability and Validity	The reliability of behavioral measures is not usully a problem. The reliability, however, rests on whether or not the behavioral indicators are the true referents. This is a question that must be argued logically.

Directions

There are seven steps in using a monitoring design:

1. Specify the problem or events of interest.
2. Specify specific observable indicators of the problem.
3. Establish who will record the measurements and how.
4. State the expected outcome in terms of the measurement.
5. Gather the data.
6. Analyze the data.
7. Adjust the measurement and/or intervention as indicated by the data analysis.

Suzette is a child guidance counselor who routinely assesses her skill by means of single-subject outcome studies with herself as target.

Suzette Young works for KIDS, Inc., a child guidance clinic in Oakton. She has worked there for 15 years since completing her M.S.W. Her job is to provide early intervention with children the school system has identified as having potential behavior problems. She works primarily with first and second graders and their families. KIDS' philosophy is that when children are having problems in school there is a need to intervene in the home situation. They work with the classroom teachers to identify specific areas where the child needs help, and then they try to involve the family in helping the child develop skills in this area. These interventions often involve learning games that parents and older siblings can play with the child.

Christine Wilder was referred to KIDS because she acts out and is distracting to other children whenever her third grade class is doing any reading activity. The school has tested Chris and determined that she does have a reading problem. Both Suzette and the classroom teacher believe that the acting out is Chris's way of avoiding reading, which is apparently extremely difficult for her. They believe that if they can help Chris read on grade level most of the behavior problem will be solved.

As a first step, Suzette has arranged for Chris to be evaluated by Carol Green, an expert in reading disorders. Carol's findings are that Chris has a mild dyslexia and that it is very difficult for her to sight-read because she sees mirror images—letters or sentences are reversed. Carol has recommended that Chris be helped to develop a phonetic vocabulary and that little effort be made to develop her sight skills. Carol and Suzette have developed a game in which Chris is asked to associate words with pictures. The goal is to teach Chris to read whole words and to learn them by associating them with pictures. Since Chris's family has limited financial resources and since KIDS budget is restricted, Suzette has decided to undertake the treatment herself with the assistance of the family rather than to hire Carol as a tutor.

Because Suzette believes strongly that many young children mask learning problems by becoming behavior problems and because she wants to encourage KIDS to develop more programs that involve parents in tutoring children with learning problems, she has decided to use Chris's case as a first case to demonstrate the efficacy of this technique. She sees this as a chance to demonstrate that she can use this technique to change classroom behavior.

Suzette obtained from the school a list of third grade vocabulary words and found pictures to represent each word. She then developed a set of flash cards that had a word on one side and a picture to represent the word on the other. She enlisted Chris's mother to spend at least 20 minutes each evening going through the cards with Chris. She was to show Chris the word, have Chris pronounce it, and then show Chris the picture. On alternative nights she was to show Chris the picture and have her pronounce the word. When Chris began to show some mastery of the words, she was to show her the word and have Chris draw the picture. Finally, when Chris was successful with most of the words they were to begin reading together. When they came to any word that Chris could not identify, they were to stop and find a picture to identify the word. They were also to keep a chart on Chris's bedroom wall on which they were to note the number of words Chris identified on the first trial

FIGURE 4.1. Chris's word recognition score across 30 days.

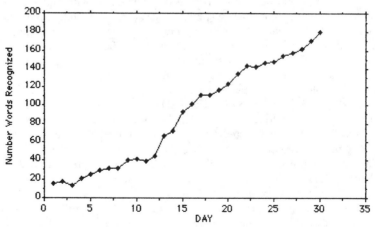

each day. This chart (Figure 4.1) shows Chris's progress. Suzette asked Chris's teacher to keep a record of how often Chris was disruptive during the intervention. In addition, she asked that the school do nothing different in terms of disciplinary action for the next 2 months so that she could monitor the impact of her intervention. When Suzette constructed a line chart of Chris's school behavior (Figure 4.2), she had a clear picture of the effect of her intervention. Based upon Chris's improvement in reading skills and behavior in the classroom Suzette concluded that this was an excellent approach for her to use and began using it with other clients with similar problems.

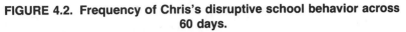

FIGURE 4.2. Frequency of Chris's disruptive school behavior across 60 days.

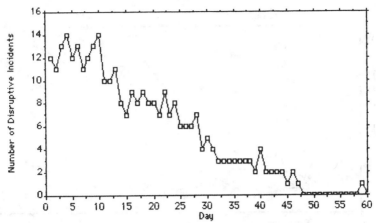

Patty works with emotionally disturbed children in a mental health center. She also routinely assesses her skill by means of outcome studies, but with the client as the target.

The Simmons family was referred to the Albright Clinic by the Central School System because the youngest son, Gregory, was increasingly a discipline problem in the classroom. The teacher, Ms. Lernwell, stated that Greg rarely did his work and often disrupted the other children by making strange noises. The most recent incident had involved Greg claiming that he had the power of levitation. He had dropped books on the floor several times and asserted that he had levitated them. They only fell, he asserted, because Ms. Lernwell had interrupted his concentration. Greg has an older sister named Gwendolyn, who everyone believes is as near perfect as is possible for a nine-year-old.

Patty Merrill, ACSW, was seeing the family. She was concerned that the two children were not talking during the therapy sessions. A review of her process notes for the first four sessions revealed that almost every time one of the children was asked a question, one of the parents would answer. Patty decided she would ask the children more questions and would stop the parents from answering by interrupting and saying, "I would like to hear what Gwen (Greg) has to say." To monitor the effectiveness of this intervention, she selected a monitoring (BBB) design. The dependent variable was operationalized as the number of minutes each child talked during the session. Patty measured this variable by timing each child's speech on the audiotapes she made of the sessions. Figure 4.3 shows the results.

In looking at the line chart, she saw that the intervention had been effective for Gwen, but she realized that she would have to find a stronger intervention if she wanted Greg to express himself.

Since the rest of the family seemed to be getting involved in the therapy process, Patty Merrill decided to focus on Greg. She chose to continue blocking other family members from speaking for Greg. In addition, she began

FIGURE 4.3. Number of minutes Gwen and Greg spoke during six sessions.

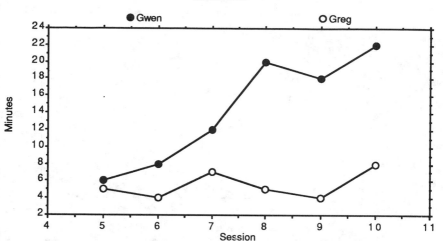

focusing her attention on him and verbally rewarding him by saying, "Thank you, Greg, I am really glad to hear you say . . . (she then paraphrased what he had said)." Patty hypothesized that this verbal reward would increase the number of times Greg spoke in the sessions. To test this hypothesis she discreetly tallied the number of times Greg spoke to her on a small pad on her desk. The first two sessions (sessions 11 and 12) were baseline sessions in which she tallied but made no intervention. She began her intervention in session 13 and continued through session 16 by blocking and verbally encouraging. This is a quasi-experimental design. Her hypothesis was that as family members were blocked from speaking for him and if he was verbally rewarded for speaking, Greg would address her more frequently. The following line chart (Figure 4.4) shows the results. While it was important to the process to get the children talking, the focus of the therapy was on the family. After session 3, Patty had identified three problem areas that the family wanted to improve:

1. *Marital distance*. Sam and Betty seemed unable to find a comfortable way to deal with intimacy and distancing in their relationship. Patty chose as a measure of this problem a marital satisfaction scale. This scale is a rapid scoring measure with several parallel forms so it can be given often without carryover effects. It yields a score of effective marital distance control ranging from 0 to 20.

2. *Parental control*. Greg and Gwen were very effective at manipulating Sam and Betty. Patty felt the parental subsystem needed to be strengthened. She measured this problem by asking the family members what percentage of parental decisions had been made as a joint decision in the last week. She recorded Betty and Sam's estimates and used an average of the two.

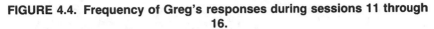

FIGURE 4.4. Frequency of Greg's responses during sessions 11 through 16.

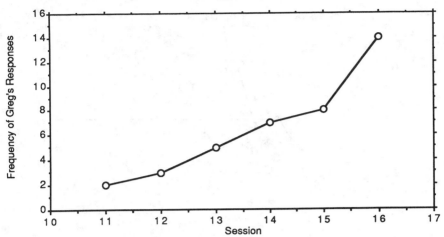

3. *Motivation to change.* The family seemed to want to talk about problems but put no effort into changing. The measure selected was the number of times Patty observed changes in behavior in the therapy sessions. Since problem three seemed most crucial to effective therapy, Patty focused her efforts on teaching the family how to change using role plays of actual situations reported by the family. Session 4 was primarily a contracting session, but baselines were begun on all three problems. The treatment went as follows: sessions 5 through 8 were focused on the idea of change with role plays, sessions 7 through 10 were focused on parental control, sessions 9 through 14 were focused on the marital subsystem, and sessions 15 through 17 were focused on change again. The results of these interventions are reported in Figure 4.5. Because the measures were in different units, they were transformed to z scores.

All measures indicated an improvement, and Patty began to define the next set of problems to work on with Sam and Betty. As the family improved, the school reported major improvements in Greg's behavior.

Brian is the social worker for Pineacre's Public Health & Nursing Department. Brian does a monitoring project to assess the degree to which his case management project is coordinating services to client families.

Pineacre has six hospitals, five private and one public. The hospitals all do an excellent job of discharge planning, but it has been evident for some time that good discharge planning is not enough. The circumstances of outpatients—

FIGURE 4.5. Simmons' family scores on three measures across 17 weeks.

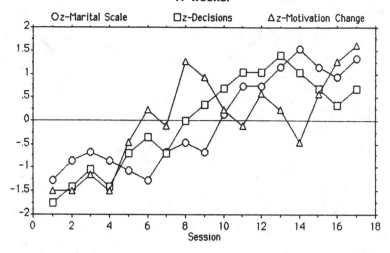

FIGURE 4.6. Brian's combined billing and survey form.

Patient Name	Account Number	Billing Date	Date Due	Physican

Mr. Clyde Client
2415 Broadway
Pinceacre, 43567

Insurance Plan	Balance Due

Date of Service	Service Code	Charge Description	Unit Price	Amount	Comment

==

Please Return this Portion with Your Payment

How satisfied are you with your Treatment Team?	Completely	Somewhat	Not at All

Do the Team Members know what each other is doing?	Always	Sometimes	Never

Do the Team Members get along with you and with each other?	Always	Sometimes	Never

Payment Enclosed $_____

especially elderly ones—often change, rendering the discharge plans obsolete. The problem is that there is no monitoring of frail elderly at home.

Last year the City of Pineacre decided to develop a case management project within its Public Health & Nursing Department. The purpose was to monitor the discharge plans of recovering or chronic elderly living at home and to provide a structure through which community agencies, home nursing agencies, and volunteer programs could coordinate their services to their clients. Funding was obtained from the Area Agency on Aging and from a private foundation maintained by the insurance industry.

Brian was appointed director of the program last year. He has gotten the interagency agreements signed that are necessary to get the "community teams" established and has written operating procedures for the teams. He has written rules for referrals to the project and has sought and received cooperation and support from participating organizations. In short, it has taken a year but all the development work has been completed. Except for one task; Brian wants to initiate a monitoring system that will give him timely feedback on whether the project is working as it should.

In designing the monitoring system, Brian reasoned that the major purpose of the project is case coordination and that the best source of information is the client. Brian wrote three questions in such a way that they could be printed on the portion of the monthly statement (Figure 4.6) that is returned by the client with his or her payment.

When 6 months' worth of invoice stubs had accumulated, Brian had responses from 30 clients. He decided to aggregate them into a summary report. First he coded each individual response (Completely/Always = 3; Somewhat/Sometimes = 2; Not at All/Never = 1) and entered them into a microcomputer using Excel©, an electronic spreadsheet. Next he aggregated the individual scores by having the spreadsheet compute the mean for each of the three items for 6 months. Last he asked the spreadsheet to put the data into a bar chart format (Figure 4.7). Looking at the chart, Brian saw immediately that all

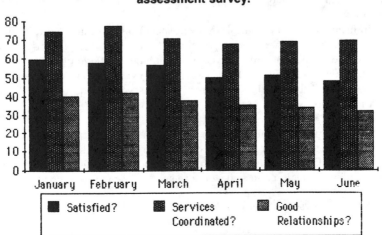

FIGURE 4.7. Brian's bar chart showing client response to assessment survey.

the scores had improved slightly over the 6-month period. The disturbing finding, however, was that although clients were reasonably satisfied with their in-home services, they did not feel they were well coordinated. Brian realized that the project would have to improve its task integration, and he set to work developing an in-service training component for team members. And, of course, he continued to monitor the program.

> *Bud is director of a child guidance clinic which has just been through a state audit. He must implement a new record-keeping system and train his workers to use it. He designs an study with his staff as target to test whether his training was effective in getting the staff to use the new system properly.*

Bud Simmons is director of the Fairview Child Guidance Clinic, a large multi-purpose program attached to the Fairview Community Hospital. The Clinic was visited by state auditors, and Bud has been told that the agency's records are not specific enough to meet the new state standards for Medicaid reimbursement. Bud has a new client information system on the drawing board because he knew this mandate was coming. Within a couple of weeks he was able to send the following memo to his staff:

Memo

To: All Staff
From: Bud

We are being required by the state agency to revise and improve our client information system. Part of the new standards require a higher level of detail in regard to client information. It is very important that we comply with these new regulations.

We will have in-service training *next Friday, March 21st,* on our new computerized client information system. It will be implemented starting *Monday, March 31st.*

In using the new system, please be as specific as you can in writing client problem statements, intervention plans, and expected outcomes. This also includes those of you who are involved in consultation and education services.

Beginning in May we will be conducting an evaluation of the system, and some of you will be asked to participate. I thank you ahead of time for your effort in this necessary endeavor.

Bud's purpose in doing an evaluation is to test the effectiveness of his in-service training. He has a subsidiary question: are the "old-timers" more resistant to changes in operations than are newer, more compliant staff members? Bud decides to monitor the staff's performance for 2 months after installation of the system.

After some thought Bud decides to use a single-subject monitoring design. He chooses at random one staff person who has been at the Clinic for more than 10 years and one who has been there less than 2 years, and each week for 4 months he randomly chooses one of their case records. He hires two consultants familiar with Medicaid regulations to do the evaluation. The first consultant reads the two records (with names deleted) each week and scores one point for each specific behavior cited and one point for each specific event cited. The second consultant reads the same two records and evaluates them on a scale of 0 to 10 on the usefulness of the information presented (the question is "If you had to take over the case today, how useful would the case record be?") and on the degree to which the record meets the requirements.

At the end of the monitoring period he adds the two scores together and enters the summative scores into a spreadsheet that produces a line chart (Figure 4.8).

The data are quite helpful in demonstrating to Bud the effects of the training. It appears that the older worker is indeed more resistant, much slower to utilize the new system properly. On the other hand, although the newer staff person picks it up more quickly, it appears that she tires of it or becomes bored with it and does not sustain her initial outstanding performance. Bud realizes that overall the training has had the desired effect, but that he should have periodic reinforcement sessions, especially with the newer staff.

FIGURE 4.8. Bud's line chart of staff scores on case records for 16 weeks.

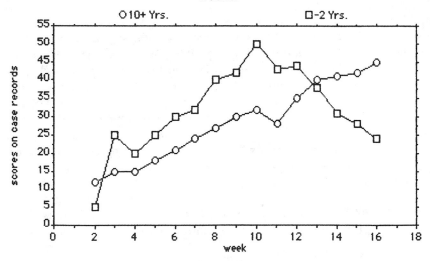

BASELINE DESIGNS

This is a design that uses quantitative methods, allowing the investigator to assess general impact and/or assess the impact of specifically planned interventions. By specifying behavioral indicators, measuring them during a baseline (no intervention) period, and stating a specific intervention along with expected outcomes, this design allows clear assessment of effects, and in some cases fairly strong causality arguments (Jayaratne & Levy, 1979; Kazdin & Hartmann, 1978).

This is actually a class of designs, all of which have one or more baselines (A) and a period that monitors one intervention effect (B), or many effects (C,D,E, etc.). The most common designs are AB, ABA, ABAC.

The advantages of this method of self-assessment are many. Compared with group experimental designs, it is fairly easy to implement. It allows for multiple interventions with multiple problems that may be evaluated simultaneously. In some instances, utilizing these designs may actually aid in the treatment or intervention itself. For example, asking a couple to monitor their behaviors after an argument may heighten their mutual awareness.

There are also a number of disadvantages. It is possible that rather than aiding the intervention, the monitoring process may hinder it. These designs can be cumbersome and difficult to implement, especially in settings where there is no opportunity to get a baseline (e.g., emergency services and brief services). Further, there is a controversy surrounding single-subject experimental design: Can this design really be considered experimental (meet the requirements of science) without the use of random selection and assignment of clients?

Random sampling is the central assumption of nearly all inferential statistics. It assures internal validity, the bare minimum, without which results are meaningless. Without internal validity, you cannot know whether your intervention was responsible for the client's change or whether change was caused by other unidentified variables (Campbell & Stanley, 1966). Validity is obtained because in a random sample each person in the population has an equal probability of being chosen for the sample. In other words, randomization removes bias from the sample. For example, from a population containing people with factor A and factor B, it is likely that a random sample will have these factors in the same proportion as the population from which they were drawn.

Internal validity, therefore, means that:

- If extraneous factors are randomly distributed among clients in intervention and control groups, and if there is client change in the intervention but not the control group, then you can be quite sure it was the intervention and not extraneous factors causing the change.

And external validity means that:

- If the random sample is similar to the population, then you can be sure that intervention will also be effective in the population at large.

Many have argued that randomization can be approximated in baseline experiments (Bloom & Fischer, 1982; Hersen & Barlow, 1976; Kratochwill, 1978). When there is only one subject—be it yourself or the client—you obviously cannot randomly select or assign that one subject to treatment and to a placebo. There are ways, however, of using the randomization idea if the intervention effect is reversible:

- *Randomize the Phases*. Rather than always administering the baseline phase before the intervention phase, determine randomly which phase will come first (with the BA design a third B phase would be added). With many replications of the study, half of the clients would be expected to receive the AB order and half the BAB order.
- *Randomize the Observations*. If there are to be 30 measurement points, randomly assign half to follow the intervention and half to follow no intervention. Under this condition, the random assignment of different time intervals to different conditions makes the observations statistically independent.
- *Use Complete Reversal*. The ABAB design reduces the likelihood that the passage of time per se is the cause of the client change, since each phase appears both early and late in the study. If the behavior returns to baseline in a third phase, then reverses again in the fourth phase, time cannot be a "plausible rival hypothesis."

Obviously, the use of these methods of approximating randomization are limited because many social work practitioners do not work with reversible interventions. We include these ideas here, however, because this possibility should always be considered when deisigning your self-assessment study.

When withdrawal is not possible due to ethical concerns or the non-reversible nature of an intervention, there is still one excellent means of showing effect:

- *Multiple Baselines*. If you are working with multiple clients/client systems, then effect may be demonstrated by assigning one client (or more) to one intervention, assigning another (or more) to a second intervention, and assigning a third (or more) to no intervention. This is an ABA, ACA, AAA design—similar to the one used by Sally in Chapter 1. This design probably approximates most closely the requirement of randomization.

Elements Required

Problem Statement?	Yes. Successful implementation of these designs is dependent upon a clear and precise statement of the problem(s).
Goal Statement?	Yes. To state the experimental hypothesis requires stating the goal of the intervention. It also requires qualifying the goal.
Observable Outcomes?	Yes. In stating the procedure to be followed and operationally defining the measures, you must state the expected outcome(s) and the observable measure of the outcome.
Measurement Tool?	Yes. There are many standardized scales and assessment tools that can be used with this design, but they are not a requirement. Instead, the tool may be a simple form on which to record a count of specified behaviors or events. The requirement of single-subject experimental designs is that the measurement tool must be individualized to the design; it must measure the referent of expected outcome.
Intervention Method?	Yes. This design requires that the intervention be conceptualized as the independent variable and be consciously introduced with discipline and care at a specific point in the intervention process. If multiple interventions are to be used, they must all be specified.

| Multipurpose Design? | Yes. These designs can be used to assess outcome and process. You must specify the area of interest and the observable indicators to be used. |
| Reliability and Validity? | Both reliability and validity can be assessed within the framework of the design. This is achieved by using multiple indicators of the problem. |

Directions

1. Specify problem(s), interventions, and expected outcomes.
2. Operationalize each. State specific observable measures of problems, specific interventions in behavior terms, and specific outcomes in terms of problem measurement.
3. State the hypothesis: the expected impact of the independent variable (the intervention) on the dependent variable (the problem).
4. Design the experiment. Specify the time period for baseline(s), the time frame for intervention(s), and who is responsible for the monitoring and creating a monitoring form if a standardized one is not being used.
5. Commence the experiment and collect data as specified in the design.
6. Analyze the data.
7. Share findings with relevant parties to the experiment.
8. Adjust intervention based on findings and repeat process.

Carolyn is supervisor in a residential facility for delinquent boys that has just added a new cottage for girls. She believes the treatment modality that has been used successfully with boys will not be effective with her girls. She tests this hypothesis with a single-subject outcome study.

Carolyn Jamieson has been a social worker at the Birchwood school for 10 years. The school accepts boys between the ages of 11 and 16 who have been adjudicated delinquent. The primary treatment modality used at Birchwood is behavior modification, and the program is successful as measured by its recidivism rates compared with other residential facilities.

  Recently Carolyn was appointed supervisor of a new cottage that houses delinquent teenage girls. She was concerned that a behavior modification approach will not be effective with these girls. The work of Gilligan (1972) indicates that women tend to be more internally controlled and, therefore, that they will be less amenable to behavioral treatment, at least as it is carried out at Birchwood.

Carolyn considered doing a large-scale study to test whether girls respond differently than boys to a behavior modification approach. She realized, however, that the new cottage will serve only eight girls, and they will be in treatment for at least a year. Because of this fact, she decided to use a baseline design with each girl serving as a single subject. Her hypothesis was that in a behavior modification program girls will show less change than boys.

Birchwood uses a system in which children receive tokens for positive and/or expected behaviors and lose tokens for negative or unacceptable behaviors. Tokens are required for participation in activities, to pay for visits with friends and parents, and to purchase luxuries such as tapes and games. A record of each child's daily token gains and losses is kept on a microcomputer spreadsheet and a line chart is printed out once a week. One line shows tokens gained through positive behavior and the other represents tokens lost through negative behavior. If a child's behavior is improving there will be increasing space between the lines. The cottage staff use these charts as a method of feeding information back to children about their behavior, children who can "swim between the lines" are praised.

Because Birchwood has been using a behavior modification approach with boys for nearly 10 years and has recorded the results, Carolyn was able to produce a line chart that depicts the average pattern of boys' response to the program. This graphic is shown in Figure 4.9, which shows that during the first 25 to 30 days token gain and token loss is variable—the two lines cross frequently because the child is testing the system and learning the rules. This

FIGURE 4.9. Average token loss and token gain among Birchwood boys.

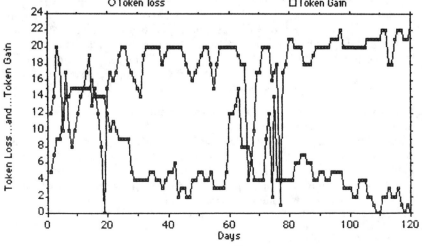

phase the staff thinks of as the baseline because the boy's behavior is reflective of his behavior at home and the intervention has as yet had no effect. Next there is a period of about 60 days in which the child does well and the token gain line runs well above the token loss line. Next, coinciding with the child's first weekend home visit, there is a turbulent period of 15 to 20 days when the two lines approach each other and often cross. During final phase the child usually settles into the program and the number of tokens gained is greater than the number lost.

In the Birchwood adaptation of behavior modification, the behaviors that lead to token gain and loss are individualized for each child based upon that child's specific needs and problems. Carolyn's concerns are not with behavior modification as a treatment, and she does believe that token gain and loss is a valid indicator of behavior change. She suspects, however, that behavior modification will have a differential effect on this new population of girls. Specifically, Carolyn hypothesizes that girls will have a longer period of adaptation and will not develop the stability that boys develop in the program. Because Carolyn's statement of the problem and hypothesis concerns differential outcomes, Carolyn knows that she must do an outcome study.

Julie is a sixteen-year-old white female who was admitted to Birchwood under court order and has a history of involvement with theft and drugs. She is the oldest of three children and comes from an intact middle class-family. The most recent problem and the reason for her placement is a case of breaking and entering in which several thousand dollars worth of jewelry was stolen.

Carolyn decided to test her hypothesis by comparing Julie's progress to the average pattern for boys as shown above. Figure 4.10 is the chart of Julie's

FIGURE 4.10. Julie's token loss and token gain for 120 days.

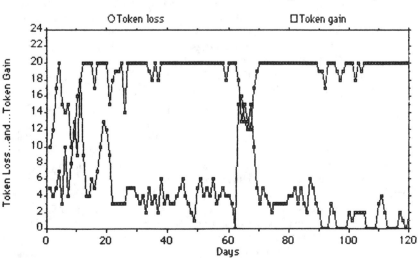

first 120 days at the Birchwood Girls Cottage. This graph shows that Julie's chart follows the general pattern for boys. Much to her surprise, Carolyn observed that Julie's response to the behavior modification program was very similar to the average of the boys' responses. In fact, it appears that behavior modification was more effective with Julie than it had been with the boys. Carolyn concluded that she would use the Birchwood program in the Girls Cottage and would continue to record and analyze the outcomes.

> *James Wilson works with abused children and their families at Pineacre Home for Children. He has been working in this capacity for 6 years and has had good success reuniting abused children with their families. For the last 3 years he has specialized in shaken baby syndrome children.*

Jim works with the children in his caseload to help them deal emotionally with the abuse and to encourage them to do whatever exercises are necessary to compensate for the physical disabilities they have suffered. He works with the foster families to help them develop the skills necessary to help their children, and he works with the natural families to help them develop appropriate parenting skills. The goal of all his interventions is to reunite families.

Jim has been very successful and has reunited 70% of the families he has served. One particular case, however, is not going well. Tommy is a four-year-old who was removed from his mother's home when he was 2. The abuse occurred between the time Tommy was 1 and 2 and he has some brain damage, although recent medical reports indicate that this may be minimal. The vision in his left eye is also restricted, and there is some question as to whether it will ever be functional.

Both Tommy and his mother have been making good progress with Jim's help until recently. In the past 2 months Tommy has shown some regression, has refused to do his eye exercises, and throws tantrums when he is required to wear a patch over his good eye to strengthen his damaged eye. His mother has become increasingly distant from Jim, has missed two of her last four counseling appointments, and has seemed somewhat distant from Tommy during their last few visits. The foster mother has been reporting that Tommy comes home from visits very agitated. In short, Jim feels that everything is going wrong in this case. Before he transfers the case to another worker, he decides to analyze his notes to determine whether he can do something differently.

As Jim thinks about the case and reads back through the record, he realizes that there has been a power struggle going on between the foster mother and the natural mother. After the foster mother had had Tommy for 6 months, she expressed a desire to adopt him, saying the mother should never have Tommy back. Jim had viewed this as a peripheral issue, but as he looked at the case he began to understand why the foster mother seemed to focus on what were normal developmental issues and take them as evidence that Tommy was not developing properly. Jim realized that she always put his eyepatch on him when she sent him to a visit even when he was in the cycle where he was not supposed to wear it, and she often seemed to induce Tommy to misbehave on visits with his mother. Jim also realized that the mother reported every minor scratch of Tommy's in order to demonstrate that the foster mother was not a good parent. Armed with this realization, Jim shifted his intervention.

He believed that if he could enable the mother and foster mother to make friends he would have to deal with fewer complaints and that Tommy's behavior would improve. He decided to get the two mothers together for a half hour per week and would engage them both in a process to help them resolve their differences. He selected three measures: the number of complaints the foster mother made about the natural mother when Jim picked Tommy up for his weekly visit, the number of complaints the mother made about the foster mother when Jim picked Tommy up to return him after the visit, and the number of times Tommy kissed his mother during the first 5 minutes of the visit. Jim felt that this last measure would tell him how Tommy was feeling about his mother.

Because he realized this kind of problem occurred in many of his cases, he wanted to assess the effectiveness of this approach. He decided to take a baseline measure for 6 weeks, do therapy with the two mothers for 12 weeks, stop therapy for 6 weeks, and do therapy for another 10 weeks. At the end of this time, he would assess the situation and decide what else might be done.

When Jim made a line chart from his data (Figure 4.11), he saw clearly that the complaining behavior of both mothers had dropped dramatically during the first intervention period. Further, he could attribute this change to his

FIGURE 4.11. Outcome of Jim's interventions with Tommy, his foster mother, and his natural mother.

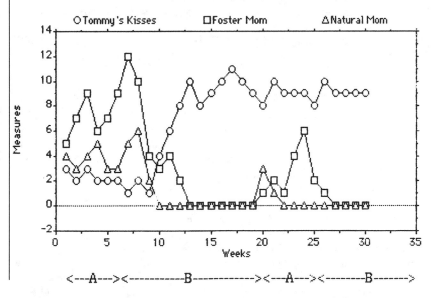

work with the family because when he withdraw the counseling session in the 19th week the behavior returned. He concluded, however, that even during the reversal period the two mothers dealt with each other and did not triangulate Tommy because Tommy's behavior showed little change during the reversal. Jim decided to document another case using this design.

> *Sam was a community organizer in Central America. She designed and implemented an outcome experiment focused on her ability to empower the community to carry on without her.*

Samatha (Sam) Smith, a community development specialist for the World Bank, had been working on a community project in Honduras for 2 years. She had helped to build a very strong commitment in her village to residential sanitation and then to community-constructed housing. Weekly meetings of the community organization were well attended, and members were very willing to raise problems and propose new ideas for solving community problems. In addition, a group from the village always attended regional meetings to monitor events that might be of importance to the project and to speak out on issues affecting the village.

Sam felt that her work was nearly done in this project and was considering asking for a new assignment. Since she was heavily invested in the project, however, she wanted to be sure that her leaving wouldn't reduce the effectiveness of the organization. To see what effect her leaving would have she developed an intervention she called *phase-out*:

- first 5 weeks she would made no changes (baseline)
- next 2 weeks she would sit at the back of the room rather than at the head table during community meetings
- next 4 weeks she would speak at meetings only if directly asked a question
- next 8 weeks she would attend only one community meeting a month
- next 4 weeks she would remain in the community but take no part in any activities

Before she implemented her phase-out intervention, Sam had to select indicators representing success of her plan. She reasoned that if the organization had reached self-sufficiency, attendance at community and regional meetings would not dwindle as she withdrew. If attendance continued at the present levels, the community organization would go on being an effective force behind the project. She also realized these were good indicators because they were easy to measure.

As she went through her phase-out over the 23 weeks, Sam collected the attendance data and put it on a line chart (Figure 4.12).

The graphic told her immediately that she had been successful. Attendance at both community and regional meetings did not deteriorate as she reduced her involvement. Her hypothesis was confirmed, since the goal was to demonstrate no change in attendance as a result of her intervention.

Looking at the data again Sam wondered if, indeed, her leaving did have

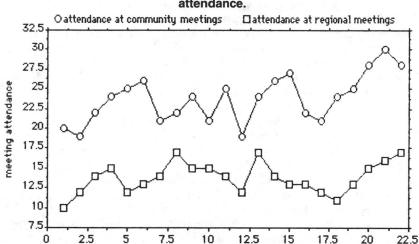

FIGURE 4.12. Sam's line chart of community and regional meeting attendance.

an impact after all. The data were variable, but it looked like there might be an overall upward trend in attendance. To test this possibility Sam used the Relative Frequency Procedure (RFP) (see Chapter 5. p. 142). She chose this technique for two reasons. First, she did not have equal numbers of observations in the baseline and intervention phases, and second, it does not require the computation of a standard deviation—somewhat difficult to do in Honduras without a microcomputer.

Using RFP showed Sam that her withdrawal had had a positive effect on community meeting attendance and that this effect was statistically significant. (Work this out for yourself using the Table of Cumulative Binomial Probability Distribution in Chapter 5, p. 143.) Increase in attendance at regional meetings was not statistically significant, but she realized that because they were usually some distance from the village there was a limit to how much attendance could grow. As a result of Sam's analysis, she felt confident that she could now ask the World Bank for a new assignment.

Caroline is a unit manager in a large field office of the Department of Human Services. She carries out a project with baseline and intervention phases to test the effectiveness of her feedback model of supervision.

Caroline Hobbs is manager of the Family Services Unit within the Child Protective Division in the Department of Human Services. Her unit is located in a large eastern city and is composed of 25 social workers specializing in intensive in-home family therapy. Within the child protection system, this unit is the last stop. Families in which child abuse or neglect has been confirmed and who are under court order are provided services by this unit for up to 1 year. If the level of family functioning has not improved sufficiently within this time frame, then termination of parental rights' proceedings are considered.

Caroline is very aware of how difficult this work is on a sustained basis. The difficulty stems from two sources. These workers are very much in the public's eye; she sometimes feels that this is one of the few professions where one may never make a mistake. The courts, and press, and the public in general are constantly scrutinizing the decisions that her workers make. Leaving a child in a home rather than foster care or returning a child home rather than seeking termination—the wrong decision can mean a child's death and can irreparably damage the reputation of the unit and the Department.

The second source of difficulty stems from the fact that the public expects rational behavior and perfect prediction from her unit, when the possibility of achieving this level of performance is very slight. The ability to be error-free assumes that the methods for changing family behavior are known and agreed upon. Caroline knows that if the means to change family functioning were readily known, then decisions could be programmed. Since the means are not known and, in her opinion, will not be for a long time, decision making requires collective judgment.

Given the difficulties inherent in the treatment of families that make up the DHS caseload, Caroline some time ago came to the realization that the quality of decision making in her unit would be in direct proportion to the quality of the job incentives her staff received from the Department. She knew that the concept of *job incentive* has two subconcepts. One is *feedback*— the quality of feedback that staff receive on their work performance. Feedback provides the worker with positive and negative external cues necessary for error detection, learning, and conformity to expected job performance standards. It also serves to prevent burnout and alienation. The other subconcept is *expectation of rewards*—the degree to which workers anticipate good performance will result in some reward. Caroline operationalized job incentives as (Van de Ven & Ferry, 1980):

- the degree to which workers know the results of their own work
- the extent to which workers perceive that doing a good job will be rewarded and poor performance will not be rewarded.

Caroline planned a training program for her supervisors that was intended to initiate a job incentive program. The objectives of the training were to teach three primary skills:

- setting concrete task objectives
- giving and receiving useful positive/negative feedback
- evaluating work performance as a consultative process

In order to assess whether the training program was effective in achieving a feedback model of supervision, Caroline also planned a baseline design with her staff as the target of the investigation. She used five items from the Organization Assessment Instruments developed by Van de Ven and Ferry (1980) and created an assessment tool for her staff (Figure 4.13). Varying the format to avoid "instrument decay," Caroline administered these items 12 times over a 2-year period—4 times before the training and 8 times after.

FIGURE 4.13. Caroline's staff assessment survey.

During the past month how often did your unit supervisor discuss your work performance with you?

never	once	4 times	8 times	8 or more

When your work performance was discussed with you, how often did you receive practical suggestions for improving your work?

never	seldom	half the time	often	every time

If you attain the performance level that is expected of you, how likely is it that you will be recognized for your good work?

no chance	small chance	50% chance	quite likely	almost a certainty

If you do not attain the performance level that is expected of you, how likely is it that you will be reprimanded or told to improve your work?

no chance	small chance	50% chance	quite likely	almost a certainty

When she was ready to do the analysis of her data, Caroline computed the scores. She decided to sum the responses to the five items, giving each administration of the survey a possible range of from 5 to 25 for each staff member. The computation finally done, Caroline now had a line chart with 12 data points (Figure 4.14) from each of her 25 staff members.

Eyeballing all 25 line charts, Caroline saw that the attitude of most of the staff had moved toward feeling that they do get adequate feedback and that expectations are concrete and rewarded. The charts did not tell her, however, whether present attitudes are really significantly different than they were 2 year ago. She could see there was a trend in the data, but because there was also a good deal of variability among staff members she could not be sure that there was a real difference.

FIGURE 4.14. Scores on Caroline's survey from one staff member.

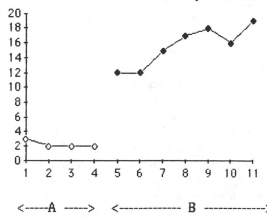

Caroline decided to analyze the data using statistical procedures. First she tested each of the 25 data sets for serial dependency and removed the autocorrelation when necessary. Next she entered each of the 25 transformed data sets into a template that she had set up to test for effect size (see Appendixes F and G). She found to her delight that her staff's attitudes had changed significantly. The percent of change ranged from 25% to 57%. She decided to continue with the in-service training program.

MULTIPLE BASELINE DESIGNS

Multiple baseline designs are two or more baseline projects combined into one study—it is the putting together of several experiments into one design. They require that the behaviors or events of interest be measured at numerous points in time and that two or more behaviors or events be monitored simultaneously. This design can be experimental if complete reversal of interventions is used.

This approach is very useful when several problems must be dealt with or when several interventions are being used to impact upon a given problem. In most social work interventions the practitioner is interested in impacting multiple problems with multiple interventions. These designs often occur naturally in the course of an intervention because you focus on one problem while simultaneously gaining information about other problems. The usual sequence is that when the first program comes under control its intervention is withdrawn and treatment shifts to the second problem. At this point—when the first intervention ceases—reversal is said to have occurred. If the problem returns, then this is evidence that the first intervention is proving to be effective with the problem. Of course, the intervention is applied a second time in order to permanently solve or ameliorate the problem and demonstrate the affectiveness of the intervention. In the case of an experiment with two interventions, the notation would be $A_1A_2B_1$ $B_2A_1A_2B_1B_2$.

The advantages of this design are many. It provides a means for monitoring change in several problems over time, and it allows the intervenor to look at how change in one problem affects another problem. It also provides a means to monitor more factors in an intervention.

The disadvantage of this design is that it requires defining one or more clear and behavioral referents. Referents, once specified and focused upon, may be reactive and change the problem simply by becoming the focus. This design, because of the need for repeated measures, can also be fairly intrusive, depending on the behavior(s) selected for measurement and the means selected for monitoring it.

Elements Required

Problem Statement?	Yes. The problem(s) or situation(s) of interest must be stated before the behavioral referents can be selected.
Goal Statement?	Yes. This method requires specification of the direction and level of change to be achieved by termination. It does not require, however, detailed and scaled goal statements as in GAS.
Observable Outcomes?	Yes. To use this method you must specify the expected outcomes and the observable measure(s) of those outcomes.
Measurement Tool?	Yes. The problem of interest and the behavior indicators that have been selected define what is to be measured. You must specify how the measurement will be recorded.
Intervention Method?	Yes. You must be specific about the interventions you will use and the order in which you will use them.
Multipurpose Design?	Yes. You can use this design to monitor clinical processes by measuring your behavior or the client/client system's behavior.
Reliability and Validity	There are several techniques to improve the reliability of behavioral observation and to assess the reliability of any given set of observations. Validity may be argued. It is a question of whether the behavioral indicators are truly referents for the problem of interest. Ajzen and Fishbein (1980) present some useful solutions to this problem.

Directions

There are seven steps in using a multiple baseline procedure:

1. Specify the problems or events of interest and decide the order in which they will be treated.
2. Specify specific observable indicators of the problems.
3. Establish who will record the measurements and how.
4. State the expected outcome for each intervention in terms of the measurement you have selected.

5. Gather the data.
6. Analyze the data.
7. Adjust the measurement and/or intervention as indicated by the data analysis.

Lena is the social worker for the Glendale Women's Shelter. Her job is to provide follow-up counseling to women with children who decide not to return to violent relationships but to live independently. Lena does outcome studies of her clients using a multiple baseline design.

Lena works for the Glendale Women's Shelter, a 16-bed facility for women and children who are victims of domestic violence. In addition to room and board, the shelter provides information and referral, advocacy, and counseling, and contracts for legal services. In addition, for women who decide to separate or file for divorce, Glendale provides ongoing support and counseling for up to 1 year after they leave the shelter.

Lena is the after-care counselor. She does home visits each week with her clients. Over the years she has developed some ideas about how best to work with this population of women. Lena's theory has to do with her function in the helping process and the sequence of changes in those functions. Lena segments treatment into thirds and adopts an different intervention role in each:

First Segment: In the third week the client is living in the shelter, Lena introduces herself and adopts a supportive role. Her goal is to reduce the client's anxiety and restore hope, self-confidence, and a feeling of personal power via the force of the client–practitioner relationship. In all interactions with the client Lena demonstrates interest, understanding, and confidence that the client can change her situation.

Second Segment: When the client has left the shelter and is living independently, Lena assumes a directive role and insists that the client focus on her child(ren). Lena's goal is to break through the client's depression, to compel changes in behavior at a time when the client is unlikely to respond to measures that rely on her own active thinking. Lena's communication is designed to suggest, advise and persuade the client to adequately care for and nurture her child(ren).

Third Segment: When the client has responded to the directive role, Lena adopts a reflective role. Her goal is to enable the client to change her behavior through understanding the failed relationship and through insight into the causative factors underlying the relationship. Lena's communication is designed to encourage self-disclosure and the ventilation of feelings.

Some time ago Lena designed a self-assessment project to test her theory about what she calls the "empowering process." She realized after she had used it with the first client that collecting the data was so little trouble—in fact, was so theapeutic in itself—that she should use the design routinely with all clients.

Lena used a multiple baseline design to investigate whether the three-

FIGURE 4.15. Lena's multiple baseline design.

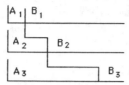

segment process was effective (Figure 4.15). She knew this was a good design for demonstrating causality because it avoids the effects of events other than the intervention effect. If specified changes in a problem occurred only *after* specified interventions at different points in time, then Lena knew she could assume a cause-and-effect relationship between the intervention and the problem. Working from her theory, Lena designed her study with three baseline phases (Figure 4.15), all starting at the same time but lasting for different lengths of time ($A_1A_2A_3$), and three interventions, all starting at different times (B_1, B_2B_3).

The first baseline (A_1) lasted for the first 2 weeks the client was at the shelter. This was the baseline because Lena had no interaction with the client during this time, but the shelter staff were able to collect the needed data for her. In week three Lena began her first intervention, the supportive role (B_1). The second baseline lasted until the client left the shelter (A_2), usually at the beginning of the fifth week, when Lena began her second intervention, the directive role (B_2). The last baseline line extended through the eighth week (A_3), when stability was achieved in the second segment and Lena was ready to introduce the third intervention, the reflective role (B_3).

Lena selected a measure representing change for each of the interventions.

First Intervention: Since the goal of the first intervention was to reduce the client's sense of being a victim, Lena constructed a simple scale to measure personal power (Figure 4.16).

FIGURE 4.16. Lena's powerlessness scale.

I feel very powerless today				
1	2	3	4	5
Am totally powerless; feel I cannot make decision; feel trapped		Feel moderately powerless		Feel not at all powerless; I control my life

Second Intervention: Since the goal of the second intervention was to help the client focus on her responsibilities as a mother, Lena chose a behavioral measure: the number of days each week the client was able to give her children a good breakfast and get them to school on time.

Third Intervention: Since the goal of the third intervention was to enable the client to focus on herself and establish a new life for herself, Lena chose another behavioral measure: the number of times per week the client did something good for herself that was educational, entertaining, or recreational.

This design produced interesting results the first time Lena used it (Figure 4.17). It turned out that all three baselines were fairly stable, and the two expected behavior changes occurred only after the onset of the intervention. The unexpected result was that the client's feeling of powerlessness did not change as a result of the supportive interaction with Lena, but rather occurred in conjunction with the client's changing behavior. The first intervention phase (B₁) showed that the client's self-perception did not improve until week 13, after the client had been taking good care of her child(ren) and herself.

These results caused Lena to rethink her hypothesis about change. She decided to continue the data collection with each of her clients, but to alter the order of the intervention roles so that she could determine if there was a

FIGURE 4.17. Results of Lena's multiple baseline self-assessment.

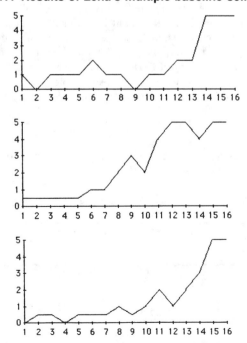

more effective sequencing. She also knew that when she had collected single-subject data on many clients she could aggregate the results to show effect size—a valuable contribution to the domestic violence field.

> *Vicky Johnson is employed by Inner City Inc. Her job is to help high school dropouts get back in school or into other educational programs. Two years ago Vicky developed a program with City Schools to work with children who are likely to drop out. The program, Victory, was designed to help children stay in school. Vicky became director with a staff of two.*

Vicky's program has three main thrusts: working with children identified by the school as highly likely to drop out, providing teachers and other school personnel with support in working with these children, and working to improve the relationship between the school and parents. Since it was started 2 years ago, Victory has been very active and has been able to involve parents in their children's education. The program is up for funding review, and Vicky wants to demonstrate its effectiveness. She can show that the dropout rate has been reduced by over 45%, and that 75% of those children they have kept in school have shown from moderate to good increases in their grades. While this is adequate evidence, she wants something that will directly tie Victory's efforts to the change in the behavior of the children in the school system.

In designing the program, Vicky had identified three variables that were strongly related to dropout rate. First was daily absence; those children who were absent 10 or more days per month were much more likely to drop out than were children with a lower rate of absenteeism. Second was grade point average; the school system operated on a 4-point system and children with a 1.5 GPA or lower were 10 times more likely to leave the system. Third was number of discipline problems, defined as the number of times the child was removed from the classroom; children who were removed from the classroom on an average of 7 or more times per week had a 95% dropout rate at age 16.

Because the school system had computerized records, Vicky was able to construct a baseline for the three measures for the school year prior to the beginning of her program. In other words, the baseline was the 9-month academic year prior to the start of Victory. She identified 150 children who had been in the Victory program (of which only 40 had left school during the 2-year intervention period), and she gathered the data about them from school records. Her data, which are shown in Figure 4.18, show the results of Victory.

In addition to the obvious change in the measures of effectiveness, Vicky noticed that each of the data sets contained interesting information. For example, there was a dramatic drop in GPAs during months 15 and 16. In trying to find out why this happened, Vicky discovered that Sally, who ran the tutoring program, had taken a maternity leave during months 14, 15, and 16. While other staff had tried to keep the program operating, they had not been able to establish the relationship Sally had with her students. Vicky realized that, in essence, a reversal had occurred and that this was even stronger evidence of the effectiveness of the program.

FIGURE 4.18. Results of Victory program showing year 1 as baseline and 2 years of program results.

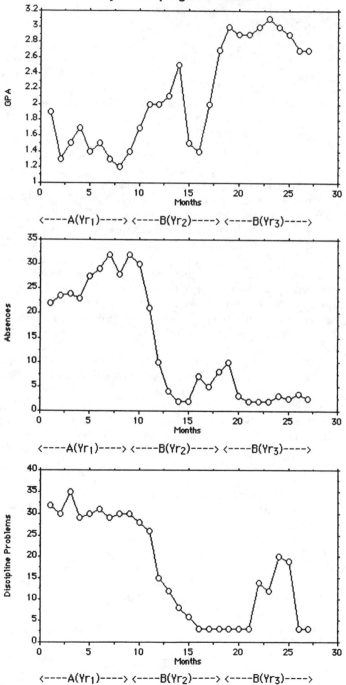

In regard to the data on absences, Vicky learned that Tom had been assigned the task of going to the local hangout at 9:00 each morning and encouraging kids to go to school. Because the absenteeism had dropped dramatically by month 14 and remained stable through month 15, Vicky had assigned Tom other duties until month 19, when it became obvious that absences were increasing fast. Again the reversal showed the effectiveness of the program.

Victory had made no direct attempt to intervene into discipline problems. Vicky had reasoned that if they helped the students perform better and if they got parents involved with the school, discipline problems would take care of themselves. Vicky was somewhat baffled, then, by the increase of discipline problems during months 19 and 25 until she realized that her staff had shifted their focus and were not paying much attention to the parents' group. A review of the notes on the parents' group indicated that during this period Victory staff had allowed them to degenerate into sessions of griping about the school system. Once the staff had refocused on parents and their needs, discipline again came under control.

Vicky found that analyzing the data in this way was very helpful, not only in providing more evidence of program effectiveness, but in providing evidence that the principles upon which she had based her programs were indeed solid. In reviewing the data Vicky was comfortable that she could defend her program.

5 Analysis of Data

Because the data collected in self-assessment studies are inherently different from that of group designs, the analytic process must be different. In most instances the number of observations will be small compared to the number of cases included in group studies. This reduces statistical power considerably. In addition, statistical analysis in group designs is based on the assumption that the observations are independent of one another. In single-system research the observations are usually dependent; an observation at time 1 predicts the observation at time 2, and thus the data are correlated. For these reasons, the practitioner doing self-assessment research cannot simply employ the techniques learned in most introductory courses in research, for these are usually applicable only to group studies.

When you collect data for a self-assessment project, you must somehow reduce their volume. Regardless of whether the data are qualitative or quantitative, reduction is the first important step in the analytic process because it is usually difficult to draw conclusions from voluminous amounts of raw data. It must first be summarized. There are many ways of doing this, but the four methods described here seem particularly useful for self-assessment designs.

The first analytic method described in this chapter is *content analysis*, a technique for coding written communication and information so that categories of terms (concepts) may be compared. Content analysis is used to analyze the data collected in case studies or whenever the data are in text form. It is favored by social workers in many settings, especially those in clinical settings where the data are contained in case records.

The second method is the *practice approach*—a functional graphic an-

alytic technique easily learned by practitioners. Practice methods use oper-
ant baseline methodologies developed by Skinner and his followers and
rely on the graphic presentation of data in the form of line charts.

The third approach is *statistical,* a method of summarizing vast
amounts of numeric data. Statistical techniques are more difficult to understand, but with microcomputers they are easily implemented and should
be used as a method of verifying the results from graphic analysis whenever
the data will allow their use.

Finally, practitioners should be able to *summarize* data from many
single-system projects in order to draw general conclusions about the effectiveness of their interventions for their client population (as opposed to
individual clients). It is through the aggregation of single-system research
projects that practice theory in social work will develop.

All four approaches have strengths and weaknesses. We will not argue
that one approach is superior to the others. Each type of analysis forces
compromises on practitioners, and it is therefore necessary to understand
the limitations and appropriate uses of each approach. For this reason, we
believe that each approach is necessary for a comprehensive understanding
of self-assessment data. You may favor one method, but you should use the
others for corroboration and when the data are inconclusive due to variability.

A WORD ABOUT MICROCOMPUTERS

Microcomputing has become a very important skill for practitioners to pos-
sess because it enables them to do many tasks more efficiently and effectively. Many social workers do not routinely use microcomputers, however, because microcomputing has been perceived as a tool exclusively for
administrators to do recordkeeping and accounting. It only recently has
been recognized that electronic spreadsheets and statistical software are
excellent tools for doing self-assessment research. Practitioners are now
seeing the potential of microcomputers.

All four analytic methods described below can be accomplished manually, but many believe that:

1. *Microcomputers are much more accurate.* If the raw scores are
    entered and verified (a simple process), graphs and statistical com-
    putations will be error-free. This is seldom true with manual com-
    putation.
2. *Microcomputers are much faster.* It is true that learning to use
    microcomputers requires an investment of time, but once it is

made the time savings are significant. It is also true that some
microcomputers require considerably less learning time than
others.

3. *Microcomputers are much less expensive than manual methods.* If
staff time is factored into the budget, over a year or two a microcomputer will pay for itself. Be aware, also, that the cost of microcomputers has been declining dramatically over the last 5 years. A
microcomputer system—including the computer unit, keyboard,
hard drive, printer, and software—can be purchased today for under $3,000.

4. *Microcomputers enable practitioners to put technology to work to
improve their practice in ways that previously were not possible.*
Microcomputers put professional accountability within the reach
of every practitioner and allow them to quickly obtain data on the
outcomes of their interventions.

Probably the most important development in the use of microcomputer technology for self-assessment is the availability of integrated software
packages. It is now possible, for example, to enter a set of numbers from a
keyboard in about 2 minutes (let us say they represent a behavioral measure taken at 15 points in time) and get back a "hard copy" graphic depic-
tion of the numbers (a line, box, or pie chart) as well as a summary statistic.
The entire process might take 3 minutes. It is this integration of data-base
management, graphic capability, and statistical subroutines into one software program that makes microcomputers so useful for doing self-assessment.

The analytic methods that follow will not include directions for manual
computation (we will cite sources when these are available). We will,
whenever it is feasible, give explicit directions for utilizing microcomputer
software to accomplish the analytic technique under discussion. Further,
Appendix F lists different types of software and the analytic techniques
they are capable of performing and describes the use of templates for ac-
complishing statistical computations.

CONTENT ANALYSIS

Content analysis is a method of drawing conclusions from data that is in
word form, be it written communication, information, or printed material
such as newspapers, transcripts, and documents. The conclusions can have
something to do with the source or sender of the message, with the message itself, or both. Content analysis can be used in many social work settings to achieve many purposes (Katzer, Cook, & Crouch, 1978; Weber,
1985). For example, it can:

- identify the psychological state of clients in clinical interviews
- reveal the focus of attention in therapeutic and task-centered meetings
- describe trends in social welfare policy evident in political speeches and platforms
- reveal cultural patterns of groups and communities in third world countries
- code responses from open-ended survey questionnaires.

Because content analysis has many uses, it should be a basic tool for all social work practitioners. Content analysis is a broad term that includes clusters of specialized methodologies. Space does not permit comprehensive descriptions for each, so we include below two examples to give the reader some understanding of its many possibilities and outline some of the major issues associated with its use. For detailed instructions and protocols please consult the list of references in the Reference section of this volume.

The basic idea of content analysis is that a text containing hundreds of thousands of words is reduced by coding so that the words are assigned to a set of mutually exclusive categories. In this way, concepts or variables of interest can be measured to determine frequency and relative importance compared to other concepts. There are many strategies for creating classifications. Basically, they fall into two groups: content classifications that you develop for yourself and general dictionaries developed by experts for manual or computer use.

Creating Your Own Classification Format

User-created classification usually focuses on one or a limited number of ideas. It permits the intensive and detailed analysis of a single theoretical construct, and the results often have high validity and reliability (Weber, 1985). If you have a clear theoretical framework, creating a classification format is not difficult. In situations where using a paper-and-pencil scale or test is difficult or not feasible—such as in therapy with a resistive or low-functioning family—then content analysis with your own classification scheme may be a very good substitute. Even when perceptual tests and/or behavioral measures are possible, the analysis of interaction via the analysis of transcripts or other documents is an excellent way of increasing internal validity in self-assessment projects.

There are six steps in developing a classification scheme and using it to analyze the contents of a text.

- Select the constructs of interest and define them clearly.

Pam was a family therapist with a family service agency. Her theoretical foundation was a family systems model. A family of three (mother, father, and daughter) was referred to her as part of an aftercare plan when the daughter (age 16) was discharged from a psychiatric hospital. The presenting problems included conflict between father and daughter, daughter's use of drugs, and daughter's depression and suicide ideation. When Pam finished her initial diagnostic assessment, she decided that the standardized scale she usually used for monitoring could not be used with this family. Instead, she would use constructs included in the scale, but measure them by analyzing the transcripts of the taped sessions. She decided to focus on indicators of the family's ability to move across boundaries and adapt to change, and their capacity to sustain warm and supportive relationships. She discussed this plan with the family and obtained their permission to tape the sessions and share the transcripts with other staff members.

- Select a unit of analysis (word, sentence, phrase, theme, etc.) to be coded.

Pam looked at the transcripts of the first two sessions with the family (these were her baseline). She realized that the speech patterns of this family were quite idiosyncratic. She decided it would not be feasible to code single words or sentences because it was often difficult to distinguish single sentences. Wanting to keep the unit of analysis as discrete as possible, she elected to code phrases.

- Define the categories. They should be mutually exclusive and should be fairly narrow (if they are too broad they don't discriminate well).

Pam was able to name her categories very easily, but the family did not seem to fit into the categories as they were defined on the original scale. She labeled the first concept "adaptability," which she defined as the indicated ability to change with changing environmental demands. She decided to rate this category on a seven-point scale ranging from "rigidity," defined as an unwillingness to change regardless of environmental change, to "flexibility," defined as willingness to acknowledge environmental change and to change with the new situation. The second category she named "relationship," which she defined as involvement or commitment to the family. She called one pole of this continuum "disengagement," defined as efforts to remove one's self from responsibility for family maintenance, and the other pole "engagement," defined as efforts to involve one's self in the maintenance of the family. These two continua became her classification scheme.

- Test this classification scheme on a document.

This study was exploratory for Pam. She had never done content analysis on a strategic intervention before, so she had to test the classification. First she had to do the coding herself to see if it worked as she thought it would. She went through the transcripts of the first session and scored each family member's statements on the two scales. She then summed the scores for each member of the family and produced an arithmetic average. The results were:

	Mother	Father	Daughter
Adaptability	6.3	8.2	10.4
Relationship	8.7	4.2	3.4

To test the reliability of the classification scheme, Pam went to two colleagues who also used strategic interventions with resistive families and asked them to code the transcript. When Pam compared the results of their coding with her own, she was surprised to find that there was 85% agreement among the coders.

- Revise if reliability is low and test again until an acceptable level of reliability is achieved.

Pam thought that the discrepancies between her coding and the coding of her "judges" were probably due to the fact that she had not provided explicit enough definitions for all points on the scales. She asked a third person to code, gave him very clear definitions for each point on the scale, and his results were almost a duplicate of hers. She decided that she could go ahead.

- Code the text(s) of interest and do a category count.

Pam completed this project by coding the transcripts from four family therapy sessions. She tallied the total number of phrases spoken by each family member and how they fell into the four categories.

Phrases Categorized by Two Concepts

	Adaptability			Relationship		
	Mom	Dad	Sis	Mom	Dad	Sis
Session 1	6.3	8.2	10.4	8.7	4.2	3.4
Session 2	7.2	6.8	9.3	6.3	5.4	4.2
Session 3	5.9	7.5	8.7	9.2	3.5	6.1
Session 4	6.0	8.2	8.4	8.5	3.0	4.7

Pam found this data to be very interesting because it gave her a way to monitor the intervention and allowed her to look at changes in a family member as others changed. For instance, as Mom became more engaged, Dad became more disengaged, and when he became extremely disengaged Sis began to show a much stronger investment in the family. As Mom showed more adaptability, Dad tended to show less. Pam concluded that the system had rules that allowed only certain levels of adaptability and engagement within this family.

Instead of coding words or phrases based on theoretical concepts, they can be coded into simple binary categories based on the text itself by using a microcomputer (Ogilvie, Stone, & Kelley, 1980). For example:

Evelyn was a community organizer trying to develop community support for programs and services to adolescents. She believed that her community's attitude toward its youth was very negative and that this was one cause of the lack of recreational and educational opportunities. She believed that if she could change attitudes, she could increase the number of youth programs. In order to test this hypothesis, Evelyn decided to do a content analysis of the local newspaper, once as a baseline and then at years 1 and 2.

Her strategy was this: Analyze the local newspaper for 1 week at baseline by coding each time the words "adolescent(s)," "juvenile(s)," "student(s)," "teen(s)," "teenager(s)," and "youth" were used in a positive, negative, or neutral context. To do this she took the seven papers to a computer facility and had news articles read by an optical scanner, a process that puts the text on a computer disk. She read the text with her agency's microcomputer word-processing program, which has a global search command. This command scrolled through the text picking out each time these six words were used. Using a split screen, Evelyn compiled a list of each occurrence of the six words, as well as the four words on each side of the occurrence. She printed the list and then manually coded each occurrence. She had another worker read the list for semantic validity.

Exerpts from Evelyn's Key-World-In-Context Analysis

Mayor Jacobs said that	adolescents	were causing problems that	negative
cost, Over 100 Mayesville	adolescents	will be pregnant with	negative
the Sheriff predicted. The	juvenile	detention facility is over	negative
security against nonstudent	juveniles	from roaming the halls	negative
Principal Green announced	students	honor assembly will be	positive
some vandalism caused by	students	is causing a delay	negative
the population of the	teenage	cohort is predicted to	neutral

Evelyn discovered that 5 of the 7 occurrences had a negative context. She took this information to the paper's editor and suggested the paper be more balanced. Evelyn repeated this analysis twice over the next 2 years and was able to document that as the content became more positive, the groups from which she was seeking support became more cooperative. Evelyn realized that although she undertook the content analysis as a self-assessment project, it also served as an intervention in and of itself. She was pleased with herself.

Using General Dictionaries

There are dictionaries available for use in doing content analysis consisting of category names, the rules for assigning words to categories, and the actual assignment of specific words. Dictionaries provide the practitioner with coding schemes with up to several hundred categories. General dictionaries have several advantages: They reduce the time commitment, standardize the results, and improve the reliability and validity. The major disadvantage is that these dictionaries have been developed for use in other disciplines such as political science and sociology, and therefore the concepts used in many areas of social work, such as in family therapy, are not included. Nevertheless, whenever your theoretical framework does not force the use of terms specific to social work, you should consider using a general dictionary for the reasons cited above.

Reliability and Validity in Content Analysis

Though there may be only one or a few categories used in self-assessment research, there is still a concern about reliability and validity. Practitioners should take care that their coding scheme is a reliable one. Reliability refers to whether the procedure is accurate and consistent. Two types of reliability are particularly relevant to content analysis.

1. *Stability*. This refers to the extent to which the results of coding are the same over time. Stability exists when the same results are obtained from the same person coding the same text more than once. If there are inconsistencies, then the coding scheme is unreliable. Inconsistencies may be due to ambiguities in the text or in the coding rules, changes in the way the coder is applying the rules, or simply to coder error.
2. *Reproducibility*. This refers to the extent to which the results are the same when coded by more than one coder. Inconsistencies between coders may be due to the same causes as cited above.

Reliability is a minimum standard for content analysis and should be calculated before disagreements between coders are resolved (for methods of calculating reliability of human coders see Krippendorff, 1980).

Validity, in content analysis, refers to the degree to which the classification scheme relates or links the concepts to their causes or consequences. To assert that a category (adaptability, for example) is valid is to assert that there is a correspondence between the category and the concept that it is supposed to represent, for example, a person's expressed willingness and ability to cross boundaries. To claim high validity, it must be shown that the same results are obtained from other data using other procedures or methods. There are two types of validity normally used in content analysis.

1. *Face Validity*. This is the weakest form of validity, but the easiest to obtain. A category has face validity if it appears to measure the construct it is intended to measure in the opinion of expert judges. In the examples above, neither Pam nor Evelyn went beyond face validity.

2. *Semantic Validity.* One way of strengthening validity is to seek
    semantic validity (Krippendorf, 1980, p. 159). A classification
    scheme is semantically valid when persons familiar with the lan-
    guage and text examine lists of words or phrases placed in the
    same category and agree that these have similar meanings or con-
    notations within the context of the study. This may, on the sur-
    face, seem to be easy to achieve. In practice, however, it is often
    difficult to achieve agreement because the meaning of words and
    phrases is often ambiguous and vague.

ANALYSIS OF NUMERIC DATA

There are many ways of analyzing numeric data. Two methods used frequently with time series designs are *graphic analysis* (the practice approach) and *statistical analysis.* The practice approach and the statistical
approach do not always yield similar results, however. It can be demonstrated, for example, that a set of data points can indicate an intervention
effect when plotted on a graph, but the *t*-statistic for the same data can fail
to show a statistically significant difference between the pre- and postinter-
vention phases. This problem is demonstrated by Gottman and Glass
(1978, p. 199) in a study that rewarded a client for controlling anxious
thoughts. Thirteen graduate students studying time-series analysis were
shown their results in graphic form (the graph is pictured below, Figure
5.1) and were asked to judge whether or not an intervention effect was

FIGURE 5.1. Line chart of number of anxious thoughts across 22 days.

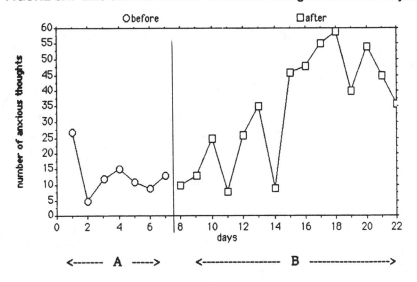

present. The data were also analyzed by approved statistical techniques (the moving-averages process described in the next section). Of the 13 students, 11 felt there was a significant upward shift between the baseline and intervention observations. When the statistical procedure was run, however, there was no statistically significant shift between the A and B phases ($t = .21, df = 19$). This example illustrates that graphs can reveal small intervention effects and make them appear to be more substantial than they really are. If a social worker was relying solely on visual inspection of these data, there would be a great possibility of accepting that an intervention effect had occurred when actually there had been no statistically significant client change.

This is an unusual example, however; the opposite is usually the case. Namely, a practitioner using graphic analysis can easily fail to detect client change and thereby assume that the intervention was having no effect. In this case, the graphic analysis would fail to expose a change in client behavior when there really was a statistically significant shift.

The point is this: "eyeballing" graphic data can produce results that vary from practitioner to practitioner and can conflict sharply with the findings of statistical tests. On the other hand, inferential statistics may be inappropriate for analyzing some time-series data, especially when serial dependency cannot be removed. Whether graphs or statistics are the most appropriate and sensitive to intervention effects is a function of many factors (e.g., the behavior or attitude being measured, the measurement procedure, the number of observations). Therefore, practitioners should not rely solely on one type of analysis but should routinely use both when possible.

PRACTICE JUDGMENT AND GRAPHIC ANALYSIS

The best argument for using the practice judgment approach (the non-statistical approach) is that the *criteria* for judging intervention effects and statistical effects are quite different. It often takes professional knowledge and skill, or practical wisdom and experience, to decide what constitutes intervention effectiveness. Take as example a child with self-mutilating behaviors, an adolescent arsonist, or a sexually abusing parent. The clinical criteria for these clients would undoubtedly require a 100% elimination of the problem behaviors, yet statistical significance could be achieved with a much smaller effect.

The second argument is that visual inspection is usually more conservative than statistical analysis. Parsonson and Baer (1978), for example, believe that graphic analysis has a built-in bias for "robust" and powerful variables. As a result of the insensitivity of graphics, they believe only basic and fundamental variables are usually detected—those possessing sufficient power and generality to be seen through graphic analysis. Undoubtedly these same variables would emerge from statistical analyses, but so too would weak and unstable variables that serve only to confound, complicate, and delay the development of theories of social work practice.

These arguments lead to the conclusion that practice judgment is most important in the early development of self-assessment in social work practice. Practice judgment assures that self-assessment research is grounded in the reality of the practitioner–client/client system relationship. Further, the emergence of basic variables, those that can be utilized by practitioners in self-assessment research, is enhanced.

Graphic analysis, however, has limitations. It is only applicable to designs that have multiple observations. Several of the illustrations described in Chapter 3 and 4 do not have the type or frequency of observations necessary for graphing data. Graphs require a minimum of three observations in the baseline and six in the intervention phase. More observations are desirable, of course, and will produce more reliable results.

Self-assessment research gathers data across time (e.g., minutes, hours, days, weeks), occasional time (e.g., successive sessions, service days), or as successive blocks of responses regardless of interresponse times. To do data analysis, data points must be plotted on a graph. The graph provides visual evidence of temporal association between changes in the target behavior(s) and the intervention.

Plots can vary enormously in terms of how "smooth" the data points are or how widely scattered they are. When there is little variability there are smooth trend lines; the creation of the graph and interpretation of the data are relatively easy, and this is the easiest method of assessing client change. The steps for doing graphic analysis are as follows:

- *Plot the data points.* This can be done manually using graph paper and pencil, or much more quickly using a microcomputer with graphic or integrated software (see Appendix D). Units of time are always on the X axis (the horizontal), and the measurement of the observation is on the Y axis (the vertical). When the data points within each phase are connected by straight lines, the result is a line chart.

David was a clinical social worker in a Community Mental Health Center. He was becoming known for his work with clients with phobias. He always charted his client data because he knew it was a means of documenting what worked and what didn't. David had a client suffering from agoraphobia, and he asked her to keep a record of how many minutes each day she was able to be away from her home. The data looked like this:

	Day	Minutes	Day	Minutes	Day	Minutes
	1	15	10	5	19	30
	2	12	11	23	20	20
	3	25	12	25	21	50
	4	18	13	30	22	20
	5	8	14	5	23	40
baseline	6	15	15	30	24	15
	7	18	16	25	25	60
	8	20	17	40	26	55
	9	15	18	10		

With these data, David created a scatterplot with the day on the X axis and minutes on the Y axis. He then connected the dots (Figure 5.2).

FIGURE 5.2. Line chart of minutes outside home across 24 days.

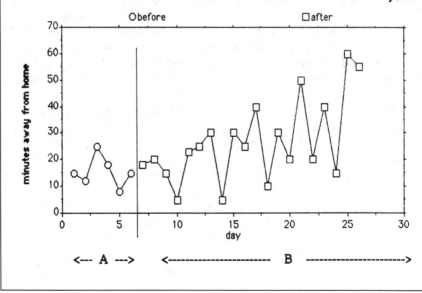

- *Analyze the results.* Line charts have a number of properties that provide information regarding the effect of the intervention. A change in the client/client system can be interpreted by means of:

Level   the point where intervention is begun and baseline ends

Slope	a linear change in the direction of the line
Drift	the absence of change across phases
Variability	the amount of scatter in the points around the line

Information can be derived from these properties of plotted data, some of which is summarized below (Behling & Merves, 1984; Jayaratne, 1978).

Changes in Level Between Phases

- Abrupt changes in level between phases are usually a convincing indication of an intervention effect.

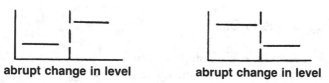

abrupt change in level   **abrupt change in level**

- Delayed, temporary, and decaying change in level between phases must always be considered a possibility. An adequate number of observations and a follow-up phase are necessary to detect these changes.

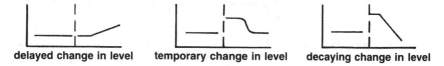

delayed change in level   **temporary change in level**   **decaying change in level**

Changes in Slope Between Phases

- Changes in slope between phases are often a strong indication of intervention effect. They can be abrupt or delayed. Change between phases is the best indicator that the intervention is producing the change. Observation must continue long enough to verify that the change is not temporary.

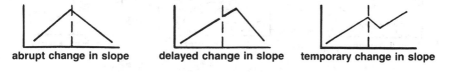

abrupt change in slope   **delayed change in slope**   **temporary change in slope**

Changes in Slope Within Phases

- Change in slope within the baseline, if toward the intervention effect, usually means the intervention effect would have been washed out if the baseline had continued. In other words, the effect was not due to the intervention but to something else. Similarly, change in slope within the intervention phase, if toward the baseline, indicates that the intervention effect has washed out.

effect will wash

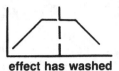

effect has washed

Changes Due to Drift

- No change in level or slope within and across phases indicates that there is no intervention effect. In other words, when baseline data drift in the direction of improvement, no claims of intervention effect can be made.

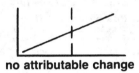

no attributable change

Variability of Data Points

As long as the graphed lines are relatively smooth, as they are above, the level, slope, and drift are amenable to visual inspection. A problem occurs, however, when there is a great deal of variability. It is very difficult to eyeball an erratic line and explain the data beyond the fact that the behavior is very unstable.

- Initial scatter followed by stability indicates that intervention control is being achieved; stable data points followed by variability indicates control is being lost; sustained scatter rules out the claim of any intervention effect.

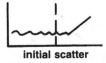

initial scatter

delayed scatter

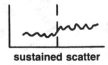

sustained scatter

There are many reasons why data points can be widely scattered. It is possible that the behavior or feeling being measured may be part of cyclical events, or it may be reflective of naturally occurring events unrelated to the intervention. It is always possible that scatter is the result of unreliable recording or measurement. Regardless of the reason, simple graphic inspection will not suffice when data are highly variable; statistical procedures are also required.

STATISTICAL ANALYSIS

Inferential statistics are based on probability theory that explains games of chance. This is such reliable theory that if the outcome of a game of chance departs substantially from what the theory predicts the outcome should be, then you are probably safe in suspecting that, indeed, it is not a game of chance at all. In other words, the outcome is not what would be expected in the natural course of things. Something (your intervention?) is having an effect.

Experiments and quasi-experiments are constructed like a game of chance. Inferential statistics are used to assess the likelihood that the intervention effect is due to your action rather than to chance. If it is unlikely that the result could have been obtained by chance, then the experiment has detected some influence other than chance—that other something being your intervention effect, if all other things are equal.

Inferential statistics allow us to calculate the degree to which we can say with assurance that it is our intervention that has produced the change rather than pure chance being responsible for this effect. If the probability of the change being due to chance is low enough (say below 5%), then we can assert that there is a relationship between our intervention and the client's change, if all other things are equal. The conclusion that it is our intervention effect rather than chance that is associated with the client change can be made if, and only if, two assumptions are met.

The first is randomization. "All other things are equal" means that extraneous factors that could account for the change have been eliminated by means of randomization—*selecting* clients and client systems randomly and *assigning* them randomly to intervention and control groups. Random sampling is the central assumption of nearly all inferential statistics. Because it was discussed in Chapter 2, the reason for this requirement will not be repeated here. Suffice it to say that randomization is an ideal that is very difficult to realize in any field of research. When any of the options listed with the description of the experimental design in Chapter 2 can be utilized, they should be. We do not believe, however, that the inability to randomize should be used as an excuse not to do self-assessment research.

The second assumption is that observations are independent of one another. Probability theory requires that each observation be independent of the preceding observations. This means that if scores show a correlation—or "autocorrelation" as it is known in time-series designs—then the statistical results will be biased.

These two requirements of statistical analysis assure that outcomes can be interpreted like games of chance in the absence of an intervention effect. The problem is that these requirements can almost never be met in self-assessment designs (nor in many social work group designs either, for that matter). For this reason, some believe that statistical analysis is inappropriate for time-series research (Campbell & Stanley, 1966).

We believe, however, that to say statistical analysis should never be used is putting the case too strongly for three reasons (Kazdin, 1976; Nurius, 1983):

- *There are methods to manage statistical requirements.* There are computational procedures developed to manage the problem of autocorrelation. These procedures test for serial dependency and then remove it by means of transformations based on "first differences" and "moving averages." It is beyond the scope of this book to explain these procedures. Please consult Bloom and Fisher (1982) for excellent descriptions of both the concepts and computations involved.
- *There are methods to deal with variation.* There are a number of procedures that, although they are based on probability theory and require statistical computation, can aid in interpreting difficult-to-read plots. Included below are directions for drawing celeration lines and graphic standard deviations and using the relative frequency technique. If serial dependency can be removed, these are very useful techniques for interpreting difficult to read plots.
- *There are methods to aid in aggregating data.* A statistical index of change, called effect size (ES), has been shown to be useful for aggregating the results of times-series designs. ES can be used for the purpose of doing program evaluation whenever serial dependency can be removed.

MANAGING AUTOCORRELATION

The problem of correlation of observations and errors is perhaps less difficult to manage than randomization. As noted above, statistical procedures assume independence. Unfortunately, most human events are linked to other events and factors, and their influence is often difficult to decompose. Further, in time-series designs we are concerned about the predictability between earlier and later stages of the *same* event (autocorrelation). This produces a problem because statistics will produce errors when the data are autocorrelated.

It is necessary, then, to test for autocorrelation before computing statistics to analyze the results of time-series studies (Bloom & Fischer, 1982). If the data are autocorrelated, then they often can be transformed to remove the dependence. If the dependence cannot be removed, then you must rely on graphic analysis, but even then you should be aware that it may be the correlation producing the effect and not the intervention per se.

Procedure for Testing for Autocorrelation

step 1 $r_k = \dfrac{(S_1 - X)(S_2 - X) + (S_2 - X)(S_3 - X) + (S_{n-1} - X)(S_{n-x})}{(S_{1-x})^2 + (S_{2-x})^2 + \ldots (S_{n-s})^2}$

step 2 Use Barlett's test to determine if data are autocorrelated:

- r_k is significantly different from 0 (is autocorrelated) if r_k is greater than $2\sqrt{n}$ where n = number of baseline observations.
- r_k is independent if r_k is less than $2\sqrt{n}$.

Although it looks forbidding, this test is actually quite simple to compute, although it is lengthy. As discussed above, it can be computed in seconds on a microcomputer once the equation is entered into a spreadsheet. Appendix F contains information on constructing spreadsheet templates. Directions for manual computation of the test for autocorrelation can be found in Bloom and Fischer (1982).

If the results of the test for autocorrelation show the data to be serially dependent, then you must try to remove the relatedness by mathematical means. There are two types of transformations, the "first differences transformation" and the "moving average transformation." Computations for these transformations are also to be found in Bloom and Fischer (1982), and templates are pictured in Appendix G.

MANAGING VARIABILITY

When data are highly variable, that is, the data points are very scattered rather than forming a clear trend line, then the data points must be "smoothed." There are a number of techniques that can be used to summarize scattered data points.

Celeration Lines

One method for summarizing scattered data is to construct a celeration line. There are two ways of drawing celeration lines. One method, recommended by Gingerich and Feyerherm (1979), is based on the arithmetic mean of the data. The other method, sometimes called the *split-middle method*, is described by Behling and Merves (1984) and is based on the median—half the points will fall above and half will fall below the line. We have chose to include this latter method first because it is the only analytic technique we know that uses the median. The median has desirable properties for summarizing this type of data because it is not particularly sensitive to highly variable and extreme scores. Because graphic packages for microcomputers do not have a celeration line function, even if you are using a microcomputer for producing the scatter plot you will have to draw in the celeration lines manually. This is not difficult.

Procedure for Drawing Celeration Lines

Step 1   Construct a scatterplot.

Step 2   Divide the plot with vertical lines: a baseline phase (A), an intervention phase (B), and other phases if necessary (C,D, etc.).

Step 3   Divide each phase in half with another vertical line such that half the points in each phase fall on either side of this vertical line (or the line goes through the middle point if there are an odd number of points).

Step 4   Determine the median point in each half-phase (i.e., if there are 4 points in a half-phase the median is between points 2 and 3; if there are 5 points in a half-phase the median is through point 3). Count the points from the bottom (the X axis) and draw a horizontal line through the median point. Count the points from the left in the half-phase and draw a vertical line through the median. Repeat for each half-phase.

Step 5   Draw a celeration line for each phase by connecting the intersection of the horizontal and vertical lines for each half phase.

The celeration line technique is illustrated on the plot below (Figure 5.3). This is the same data set that David obtained from his agoraphobic client. The data points represent the number of minutes per day the client was out of her house.

FIGURE 5.3. Illustration of celeration line technique.

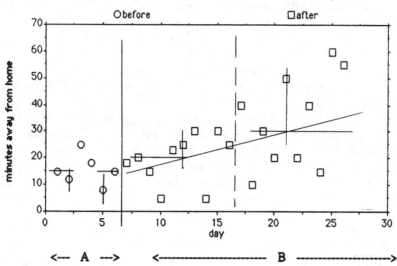

The scatter of the data points during the intervention phase in this graph is excessive. The celeration lines drawn on this plot make it much easier to interpret. They show that there is a gradual change in slope in the direction of improvement. Because of high variability, however, any conclusion regarding intervention effect should be postponed until stability is achieved.

The celeration line approach for summarizing variable data has one large advantage: You do not have to test for autocorrelation because this technique is not a statistical process relying on probability theory. However, the disadvantages are several. The number of observations in the baseline and intervention phases should be approximately the same number because celeration lines are trend lines, which are a function of time. The data used to illustrate this technique would be better analyzed, then, by one of the other methods described below. Second, celeration lines cannot be used when the baseline is bounded, meaning that the line reaches either the maximum or minimum. If it does, it obviously cannot be extended into the intervention phase.

The Two Standard Deviation Procedure

This procedure is an aid to practice judgment because it provides a guide for knowing when a client/client system has reached the goal of the intervention (Behling & Merves, 1984). The procedure enables you to put two lines on a plot so that the plot is divided into three zones: a desirable, typical, and undesirable zone. The zones are computed directly from the scores and can be done most easily on a microcomputer.

The two standard deviation procedure uses the mean (the arithmetic average) as representing the typical behavior. Whereas the celeration line uses the median point for representing the most typical behavior or attitude, this procedure designates the mean as the most typical. Because the mean is a mathematical function of every score, it is the balancing point in a distribution of scores. As such, it is very sensitive to extreme scores.

The mean by itself—single numeric value—has little meaning, however. Knowing the average behavior tells us nothing about the variability of the target behavior or feelings. The mean, for example, could be the same for the baseline and intervention phases, yet the plots could be very different depending on the amount of scatter. The standard deviation gives us parameters to judge the variability of the behavior based on the most typical behavior.

If your distribution of scores forms a normal curve (and we assume it does), then we know that 68% of all baseline scores will lie one standard deviation on either side of the mean, and 95% of all baseline scores will lie within two standard deviations of the mean. The two standard deviation procedure defines the typical behavior zone as the range encompassing 95% of the scores in the baseline phase. This range—two standard deviations above and below the mean of the baseline phase—is drawn on the scatterplot. By extending this range into the intervention phase, you create a guide for judging the extent to which the target behavior has changed between phases. In other words, whenever an observation is different enough to fall outside 95% of the baseline scores, then we take it to be an intervention effect (if, of course, it is in the right direction).

Procedure for the Two Standard Deviation Procedure

Before: Test for autocorrelation and transform data if necessary.
Step 1:   Compute mean and standard deviation for baseline phase.
Step 2:   Draw lines two standard deviations above and below the mean of the baseline phase and extend them into the intervention phase.

Step 3:   Label the zones in the correct direction (typical, undesirable, desir-
          able).
Step 4:   Count how many observations in the intervention phase fall into the
          desirable zone.

The two standard deviation procedure is illustrated on the plot below (Figure 5.4). The space between the two lines represents the typical behavior

FIGURE 5.4. Illustration of two standard deviation procedure.

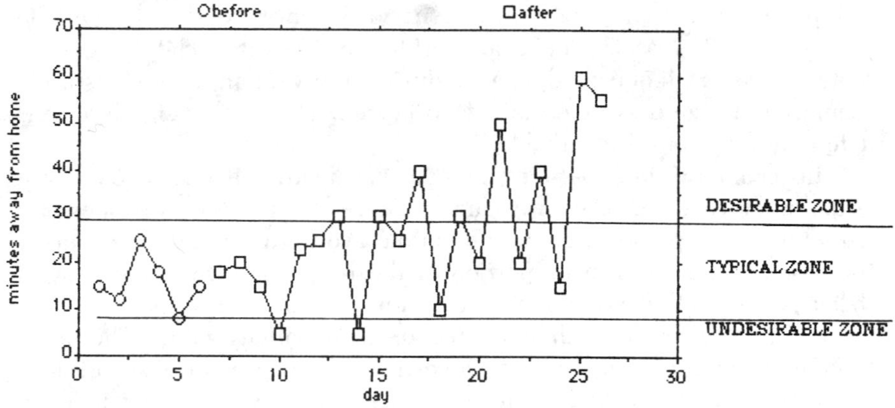

intervention. This procedure is easily done when a microcomputer is available. Using David's data set again as an illustration, the steps would be as
follows:

1.   Compute the mean and the standard deviation for the baseline
     phase using a statistical software package or a spreadsheet. In
     David's data set, the average number of minutes the client was
     able to remain outside her home during the baseline period was
     15.5; the standard deviation was 5.7 minutes.
2.   Make a printout of a line chart generated by the software.
3.   Starting at the mean on the vertical axis, draw one line two stan-
     dard deviations above the mean [the mean $+ (2 \times 5.7) = 26.9$]
     and one line two standard deviations below the mean [the mean
     $- (2 \times 5.7) = 4.1$]. Label the zones as shown.
4.   Draw your conclusions. As can be seen from David's data, two
     observations fell in the undesirable zone, 8 in the typical zone,
     but 10 in the desirable zone.

This is a relatively simple method for drawing some conclusions from difficult-to-read graphs. You do not have to consult a probability table, as you do with the method that follows. Further, because the two standard deviation line is computed directly from the data and not from the number of observations, the two standard deviation method is recommended when there is not an equal number of observations in the baseline and intervention phases.

The Relative Frequency Procedure

This procedure assumes that typical behavior is represented by the middle two-thirds of the baseline behavior (Behling & Merves, 1984). To the extent that scores fall outside this range during intervention, then statistically significant change is assumed to have occurred. The level of significance is determined by consulting a table.

Instead of two lines defining a range of standard behavior based on the arithmetic mean, the relative frequency procedure projects two lines into the intervention phase based on the middle two-thirds of the scores during the baseline period. The proportion of the behavior during intervention that falls outside this typical range in the direction of improvement is calculated. This proportion is then located on a probability table. The value taken from the probability table is the estimate of the statistical significance of the change. The relative frequency procedure gives a numeric index of the degree to which the change is statistically significant as well as graphically observable.

Procedure for Relative Frequency Procedure

Before   Test for autocorrelation and transform data if necessary.
Step 1: Count the number of observation points during the baseline period.
Step 2: Determine the typical range of the target behavior by multiplying the number of observations by $2/3$.
Step 3: Draw two lines to include the number of typical observations. At least one observation must be above and below the two lines.
Step 4: Calculate the proportion of the time a score was found in the desired behavior zone during the baseline period.
Step 5: Count the number of observation points in the intervention phase.
Step 6: Consult the Binomial Probability Table (Table 5.1) below.

TABLE 5.1. Table of Cumulative Binomial Probability Distribution

Proportion	Number of Observations											
	4	6	8	10	12	14	16	18	20	24	28	32
.05	2	2	3	3	3	3	3	4	4	4	4	5
.10	3	3	3	4	4	4	5	5	5	6	7	7
1/8	3	3	4	4	5	5	5	6	6	7	8	8
.15	3	3	3	4	4	5	5	6	6	8	8	9
1/6	3	4	4	4	5	6	6	7	7	8	9	10
.20	3	4	5	5	5	6	7	8	8	9	10	11
.25	4	4	5	6	7	7	8	9	9	11	12	13
.30	4	5	6	6	7	8	9	10	10	12	13	15
1/3	4	5	6	7	8	9	9	10	11	13	15	16
.35	4	5	6	7	8	9	10	11	12	13	15	16
3/8	4	5	6	7	8	9	10	11	12	14	16	18
.40	4	5	6	8	9	10	11	12	13	15	16	18
.45	4	5	6	8	9	10	11	13	14	16	18	20
.50		6	7	9	10	11	12	13	15	17	19	22

Table of the Cumulative Binomial Probability Distribution, By the staff of the Harvard Computational Laboratory, Harvard University Press, 1955, Table constructed under the direction of Dr. James Norton, Jr., Indiana University-Purdue University, 1973.

Again, David's data are used to illustrate the use of the relative frequency method.(Figure 5.5).

As can be seen, this method is less conservative than the two standard deviation procedure—there are more observations in the desirable zone. Here is the way to draw the bands on this plot:

1. Find the number of observations in the baseline phase (there are six).
2. Find the typical range of behavior (6 × 2/3 = 4.02).

FIGURE 5.5. Illustration of relative frequency procedure.

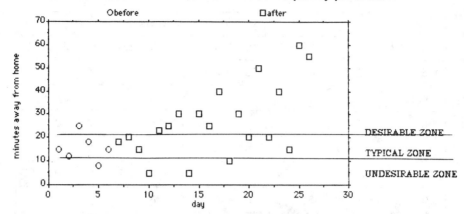

3. Draw two lines to encompass the typical range of behavior (4 scores are in the baseline; this leaves the score of 25 in the desirable zone).

4. Find the proportion that the scores in the desirable zone are of all scores in the baseline (in this case there is one score in the desirable zone so $^{1}/_{6} = .167$).

5. Count the observation points in the intervention phase (there are 20).

6. Consulting the Table of Cumulative Binomial Probability Distribution below (Table 5-1), look in the top row for the number of intervention observations (in this case 20). In the first column, find the proportion of the time the baseline observations fell in the desirable zone ($^{1}/_{6}$ or .167). Follow this row to the right until it intersects with the column identified above and take the number (in this case it is 7). Since you have 11 observations in the desirable zone and 11 is larger than 7, you can say that your results are statistically significant at the .05 level of probability. In other words, if you had less than 7 observations in the desirable zone it would not represent a significant change.

Notice that the probability table (see Table 5.1) can also be used with the celeration line method.

With both the celeration line and relative frequency methods, the number of data points needed to fall above the lines for a statistically significant effect to be present is a function of the number of observations there are in the intervention period. To the extent that the ratio of points above the line in the intervention phase is larger than in the baseline phase, then the intervention effect is significant.

The three techniques that have been described above are useful for drawing conclusions from hard-to-interpret data. They enable the practitioner to analyze differences between baseline performance and performance that is the result of an intervention. Depending on the nature of the data, you may want to rely on just one method or use all three. Either way, they are an excellent way to inform and reinforce your practice judgments.

AGGREGATING TIME-SERIES DATA

When social workers build self-assessment research into their practices on a routine basis, the time will come when they have accumulated the results of many studies. There may also be an occasion when they want to compare their results with other practitioners who use the same interventions with the same type of clients. They may also wish to test whether they can generalize the findings from their clients to larger populations (Kennedy, 1979).

New procedures termed *meta-analysis* have been designed to allow comparisons of research findings. One of these procedures is the calculation of the average effect size (*Gingerich, 1984*; *Corcoran, 1985*). This statistic (ES) has been adapted for use in time-series designs by basing the computation on gain scores—the difference between observations in the baseline and the intervention phases. The differences between these paired scores $(x_B\text{-}x_A)$—the first score of the baseline and the first score of the intervention—are summed across all the data points, then averaged, then standardized by dividing by the standard deviation of the gain score (sdg).

This statistic is most useful for time-series research because it incorporates the essence of practice research, namely, time. Because ES is a standardized score and because we assume a normal distribution of baseline scores, a Normal Curve Table of z-scores can be consulted to translate the ES into a percentage. The percentage can then be interpreted as the percent of change between the average score at baseline and the average score during the intervention. As a description of percentage of change over time, it is a very useful index for social workers engaged in self-assessment.

The use of ES as a method for summarizing the results of a single-system study and for comparing it with other studies depends on the same assumptions that we made for the other statistical procedures described above. The data must be serially independent (so you must test for autocorrelation first), and there must be sufficient data points; a minimum of seven pairs is a good rule of thumb. Equal numbers of baseline and intervention scores are not a requirement, however.

The computation of ES is not difficult; the description for manual computation is found in Corcoran (1985, p. 11). To set up a microcomputer spreadsheet to compute ES, see Appendix F and the template for ES reproduced in Appendix G-7. This statistic—the index of change between phases in single-system research—has many applications and is well worth the time investment to learn the procedure.

6 Social Work Practice and Research

We have done many workshops for social work professionals at which we teach the methodologies included in this book. Invariably, around noon a participant will approach to say that (s)he is leaving because the skills being taught are unnecessary in his/her practice. "I don't need all of this," she says, "I know when I'm effective and when I'm not."

We began this book with another opinion, a quote from Bertrand Russell (1976, p. 16), in which he acknowledges that we gain important knowledge from "genuine insight," but says that by itself intuition is not a sufficient basis for professional practice. In other words, Russell believes that wisdom gained from practice experience is "an insufficient guarantee of truth" and, if it is to be taken as such, must be tested by empirical means.

Russell's view is now the standard of the social work profession. It does not demand an abandonment of practice wisdom, but rather requires us to test this wisdom in order to verify it and make it available to others.

This book has taken a basic yet broad approach to empirical self-assessment methodology. We have included the broad range of designs and data collection methods that are available to social workers today. Yet resistance to empirical methods as advocated by Fischer (1973) continues by those who do not realize that there are methods to fit almost all kinds of practice knowledge.

It is easy to understand why this standard is encountering resistance. Social work practitioners probably face a greater challenge when they attempt self-study than is faced by many other helping professionals because of the nature of social work practice. That is why it is important to be aware that there are methods appropriate for a wide range of practice situations.

SOCIAL WORK PRACTICE

Social work has the broadest scope of interest of the helping professions (Hardiker & Baker, 1981) and is multidisciplinary in its approach (Collins, 1986). It is a field that uses a systemic approach and deals with the entire range of human problems. As a field, social work is more defined by diversity and process than by specific techniques or an identifiable knowledge base (Keister & Pfouts, 1984).

There have been many attempts to define a discrete social work domain (Compton & Galaway, 1979). Timms and Timms (1977), for example, argue that many concepts in social work cannot be defined in terms of dictionary definitions but rather must be understood in a broad contextual sense. They believe that it is probably impossible to develop one definition of person-in-situation, the most central concept. This concept, they say, defines social work as a profession that focuses upon people, environments, and the interaction between the two, and it defines social work as a field that deals with interacting systems.

When we speak of person-in-situation, then, we are defining the basic focus of the profession. We are saying that to focus on the person, as does psychology, or to focus on the situation, as does sociology, is not the framework through which we understand human problems and solutions. This approach acknowledges that the researcher also comes to the research with values, beliefs, perceptions, capabilities, and desires, and becomes part of the situation. To some extent person-in-environment implies that the situation becomes more than the sum of the parts or, at least, more than could be predicted by study of one without the other. The concept always implies that there is interaction between the two systems. The concept of person-in-situation provides a unique perspective, and we do not despair of this scope and diversity. It gives the field a unique view of the world that tends to broaden our knowledge base rather than reduce it, as is done in other social sciences.

In addition to its broad scope, there are other characteristics of social work that make it at times a challenge for the researcher. One is its multiplicity of outcomes. Social work interventions, because they involve changes in people's lives, always involve complex outcomes and are frequently designed to impact on multiple targets. Neugeboren (1985) demonstrates that a management decision or action may be planned to impact upon many different target groups and to impact them differently. A manager may be interested in having one impact upon her or his staff, a second on his or her supervisor, a third on consumers. The manager may hope to accomplish these varying impacts with one action or decision. Peters (1987) argues that not only do management decisions and actions impact all these levels, but that the impacts are interactive and that managers must learn to evaluate their performance based upon multiple impacts.

Collins (1986), in his biography of Martin Luther King, points out that Dr. King was aware of and planned his impact upon many different levels of society. Steinem (1983) argues that feminists must attack the problem of sexism at every level from the most intimate and personal to the highest level of political power. Donovan (1967) discusses the horror that went through the Johnson Administration when the staff began to realize the impact that the maximal participation clause in the War on Poverty legislation was going to have on many of Johnson's closest political allies. Alinsky (1979), in his discussion of means and ends, implies that community action needs to be aware of and plan its impact upon many levels.

Such examples are also found in clinical settings. A social worker may, for instance, be working with a client on a case plan having goals that include an impact on a family system, a work system, and other community systems. Rarely in this situation is the social worker in a position to gather data on the other systems, at least not data other than that reported by the client. Further, if one takes seriously the systemic position, then we would expect that any intervention would have an impact on a number of other systems, some of which may not be known to the social worker.

These are some of the characteristics of social work that make it less amenable to research than are other professions. We underscore three factors:

- Our insistence on "taking in" the client and the client's larger context.
- The necessity of planning for and working at multiple levels.
- The fact that most of what we do occurs in the field and not in an office or laboratory, where variables can be more easily controlled.

These factors, taken together, mean that social work is a complex endeavor. Add to this complexity the difficulties inherent in self-assessment research, and practitioners' resistance is understandable.

SELF-ASSESSMENT RESEARCH

All science is based upon observation. Until Einstein (1969) presented his theory of relativity, which argued that all observation was inherently dependent upon the vantage point of the observer, it was assumed that the trained scientific observer was objective and reported the facts of the phenomena independent of vantage point. Einstein (1969) demonstrated that the same phenomena may be judged to be quite different based upon the relationship between the observer and the observed. For practical purposes there is no absolute vantage point from which to observe.

We also know that the very act of observation can alter the phenomenon being observed, and that what one observes will be determined by the vantage point one selects and the instruments chosen for the observation (Wolf, 1989). The problem of objectivity becomes even more difficult when the object of observation is the observer, however. F.A. Wolf (1989) argues that when different observers (or the same observer using different vantage points) reach similar conclusions about a phenomena, there are sufficient grounds to believe that the event or behavior does exist in reality. She labels this reality the "out there" because it is different from perceptions that are "in there." The "out there" reality we term *empirical knowledge*.

When, however, one is observing oneself there is no "out there." In self-evaluation, when we wish to make judgments about ourselves we can theoretically establish a referent outside ourselves. The problem is that since the intervener is always part of the intervention, there is always a threat of reactivity.

To clarify this issue, consider the situation in which one wants to make a statement about the nature of a family interaction. One can observe the family and ask others to observe the same family. By comparing observations some validity can be established about this family's interactions because a reasonable argument can be made that the two observers are detached from the family being observed. If, however, I am a member (or therapist) of the family being observed, then I am an integral part of that which is being observed and it cannot be argued that I am detached from the object of observation.

Campbell and Stanley (1963) state that one threat to the validity of an experimental design is the reactivity of the instrument. The family study cited above could be planned so that the family is unaware that it is being observed or so that the family is unaware of the purpose of the observation, and therefore one could argue that the observations are nonreactive. There is no way, however, that one can observe one's self and not be aware of the observation or the purpose of the observation. Any self-observation will contain some element of reactivity.

Part of the solution to this problem may lie in the understanding of evaluation and in the purpose of self-evaluation. If, as Isaac and Michael (1981) argue, evaluation is a technological pursuit, then its purpose is to determine whether an intervention is achieving the goal it was designed to achieve. If we connect this idea with Campbell and Lee's (1988) argument that the purpose of self-evaluation is correction or self-improvement, then reactivity, far from being a problem, becomes exactly what one is seeking. If the purpose of self-evaluation is self-change, then one seeks correction as the information becomes available. This approach answers the problem to a degree but leaves unanswered the general issue of the validity of the information being used in the evaluation.

Campbell and Lee (1988), in addressing the discrepancies between self-rated performance scores and supervisor-rated performance scores, have argued that each rater is possessed of different information about the question and that there is no logical ground to argue that one is more accurate than the other. When one looks at the two sets of scores, one simply has two constructions of reality from two differing vantage points.

If we accept the position that scientific method is a process for testing and communicating personal perceptions, then the issue of objectivity simply ceases to be an issue, or, at least, we can argue that one observer's information is as useable as another's. While this to some degree answers the issue from a methodological standpoint, at some intuitive level we know that an observer who has an investment in the results is more likely to slant the information in certain directions than a disinterested observer. We are more likely to put a positive construction on our own behavior than on that of someone in whom we have no interest.

There is no way around this conundrum except to be very aware of the special risks to validity we cited in Chapter 2. On the one hand we acknowledge that reality is relative and personal, yet on the other hand the profession must search for truth to which all can ascribe. Our advice is to use multiple measures and multiple observers whenever possible.

Given the complexity of social work practice, its breadth of scope and multiplicity of levels and impacts, this text has suggested an approach to self-assessment research that is problem-oriented. One way to reduce complexity is to focus on problems and their resulting questions. Self-assessment research should be designed to gain information that can be used to create needed change. It is utilitarian. This approach seems particularly effective for social work because social workers are change agents (Compton & Galaway, 1979); they need information that will lead to change.

Self-evaluation should be a career-long process and not a discrete event or series of discrete events. If this is the case, then many methodologies can be incorporated into designs, depending upon the question of interest at a particular moment. Rather than restricting self-evaluation to a single approach or methodology, it is more enjoyable and more informative to use different techniques at different times. If we accept that social work practice incorporates varying techniques and involves knowledge from different levels, then evaluation should include an assessment of the impact of this knowledge on practice and its value or import.

The approach being proposed here could be viewed as a cake composed of three tiers. Each tier supports the tiers above it, and all fit together to form a whole. The first tier is the faith that undergirds the practice of social work. The second is the intuitive, insightful, and expert knowledge gained from experience that guides one's practice. The third is the empirical or scientific knowledge that comes from testing and verifying the first two layers. Knowledge at each level can and should be evaluated using a methodology appropriate to the types of knowledge being tested.

References

Alinsky, S. D. (1979). Of means and ends. In F. Cox, J. Erlich, J. Rothman, & J. Tropman (Eds.), *Strategies of community organization*. Itasca, IL: Peacock.

American Psychiatric Association. (1987). *Diagnostic and Statistical Manual of Mental Disorders—Revised, 3rd ed*. Washington, DC: Author.

Azjen, I., & Fishbein, M. (1980). *Understanding attitudes and predicting social behavior*. Englewood Cliffs, NJ: Prentice Hall.

Behling, J. H., & Merves, E. S. (1984). *The practice of clinical research: The single case method*. New York: University Press of America.

Bellack, A. S., & Hersen, M. (1988). Self-report inventories in behavioral assessment. In J. D. Cone & R. P. Hawkins (Eds.), *Behavioral assessment: A practical handbook* (pp. 52–76). New York: Brunner/Mazel.

Berdie, D. R., & Anderson, J. F. (1974). *Questionnaire design and use*. Metuchen, N.J.: Scarecrow.

Bloom, M., & Fischer, J. (1982). *Evaluating practice: Guidelines for the accountable professional*. Englewood Cliffs, NJ: Prentice-Hall, Inc.

Bloom, M., Butch, P., & Walker, D. (1979). Evaluation of single interventions. *Journal of Social Service Research, 2*, 301–310.

Briar, S. (1980a). Problems and issues in implementing the clinical-research model of practice in educational and clinical settings. Cited in J. R. Conte & R. L. Levy, *Journal of Education for Social Work, 16*, 62–66.

Briar, S. (1980b). Toward the integration of practice and research. In C. Fanshel (Ed.), *Future of Social Work Research*. Washington DC: National Association of Social Workers.

Brodsky, S. L., & O'Neal Smitherman, H. (1983). *Handbook of scales for research in crime and delinquency*. New York: Plenum.

Burrill, G. C. (1976). The problem-oriented log in social casework. *Social Work, 21*, 67–68.

Campbell, D. J., & Lee, C. (1988). Self-appraisal in performance evaluation: Development versus evaluation. *Academy of management review, 13* (2), 302–314.

Campbell, D. T., & Stanley, J. C. (1966). *Experimental and quasi-experimental designs for research*. Chicago, Ill.: Rand McNally.

Chernesky, R., & Young, A. (1979). Developing a peer review system. In Rehr, H. (Ed.), *Professional accountability for social work practice* (pp. 74–91). New York: Prodist.

Cole, S. (1972). *The sociological method*. Chicago, IL: Markham Publishing Company.

Collins, B. G. (1986). Defining feminist social work. *Social Work, 31*(3), 214–219.

Compton, B. R., & Galaway, B. (1975). *Social work processes*. Homewood, IL: Dorsey Press.

Conte, J. R., & Levy, R. L. (1980). Problems and issues in implementing the clinical-research model of practice in educational and clinical settings. *Journal of Education for Social Work, 16*, 60–66.

Corcoran, K. J. (1985). Aggregating the idiographic data of single-subject research. *Social Work Research and Abstracts, 21*, 9–12.

Corcoran K., & Fischer, J. (1987). *Measures for clinical practice: A sourcebook*. New York: Free Press.

Coulton, C. J., & Solomon, P. L. (1977). Measuring outcomes of intervention. *Social Work Research and Abstracts, 13*, 3–9.

Donovan, J. C. (1973). *The politics of poverty*. Indianapolis, IN: Pegasus.

Ezell, M., & McNeece, C. A. (1986). Practice effectiveness: research or rhetoric? *Social Work, 31*, 401–402.

Einstein, A. (1931). *Relativity: The special and the general theory*. New York: Smith.

Fink A., & Kosecoff, J. (1985). *How to conduct surveys: A step-by-step guide*. Beverly Hills, CA: Sage Publications.

Fischer, J. (1973). Is casework effective? A review. *Social Work, 18*, 5–20.

Fischer, J. (1978). Does anything work? *Journal of Social Service Research, 1*, 215–243.

Gert, B. (1973). *The moral rules*. New York: Harper & Row.

Gilligan, C. (1972). *In a different voice*. Cambridge, MA: Harvard University Press.

Gingerich, W. (1984). Meta-analysis of applied time-series data. *The Journal of Applied Behavioral Science, 20*, 71–79.

Gingerich, W. (1979). Procedures for evaluating clinical practice. *Health and Social Work, 4*, 104–130.

Gingerich, W., & Feyerherm, W. (1979). The celeration line technique for assessing client change. *Journal of Social Service Research, 3*, 99–113.

Glaser, B. G., & Strauss, A. L. (1967). *The discovery of grounded theory: Strategies for qualitative research*. Hawthorne: N.Y.: Aldine Publishing.

Gottman, J. M., & Glass, G. V. (1978). Analysis of interrupted time-series experiments. In R. R. Kratochwill (Ed.), *Single subject research: Strategies for evaluating change* (pp. 197–235). New York: Academic Press.

Greer, F. (1971). *The female eunuch*. New York: McGraw-Hill.

Hage, J., & Meeker, B. F. (1988). *Socialcausality*. Boston, MA: Unwin Hyman.

Hardiker, P., & Baker, M. (1981). *Theories of practice in social work*. New York: Academic Press.

Hersen, M., & Barlow, D. H. (1976). *Single case experimental designs: Strategies for studying behavior change*. New York: Pergamon.

Hopps, J. G. (1985). Effectiveness and human worth. *Social Work, 16*, 467.

Hudson, W. W. (1981). Index and scale construction: Client problem assessment. In R. Grinnell (Ed.), *Social work research and evaluation*. Itasca, Ill.: Peacock.

Isaac, S., & Michael, W. B. (1981). *Handbook in research and evaluation* (pp. 130–155). San Diego: Edits.

Jayarantne, S. (1978). Analytic procedures for single-subject designs. *Social Work Research and Abstracts, 14*, 30–40.

Jayarantne, S., & Levy, R. L. (1979). *Empirical clinical practice*. New York: Columbia University Press.

Johnson S. M., & Bolstad, O. D. (1973). Methodological issues in naturalistic observation: Some problems and solutions for field research. In L. S. Hammerlynck, L. D. Handy, & E. J. Mash (Eds.), *Behavior change: Methodology, concepts, and practice* (pp. 7–58). Champaign, Ill.: Research Press.

Jones, R. R., Reid, J. B., & Patterson, G. R. (1975). Naturalistic observation in clinical assessment. In R. McReynolds (Ed.), *Advances in psychological assessment* (pp. 42–89). San Francisco, CA: Jossey-Bass Publishers.

Kagle, J. (1984). *Social work records*. Homewood, Ill.: Dorsey Press.

Katzer, J., Cook, K. J., & Crouch, W. W. (1978). *Evaluating information*. Reading, MA: Addison Wesley.

Kazdin, A. E. (1976). Statistical analysis for single-case experimental designs. In M. Hersen & D. H. Barlow (Eds.), *Single case experimental designs: Strategies for studying behavior change* (pp. 103–125). New York: Pergamon.

Kazdin, A. E., & Hartmann, D. P. (1978). The simultaneous treatment design. *Behavior Therapy, 9*, 912–922.

Kiester, D. J., & Pfouts, J. H. (1984). The value base for social work. In A. E. Fink, J. H. Pfouts, & A. W. Dobelstein (Eds.), *The field of social work*. Beverly Hills, CA: Sage Publications, 19–32.

Kennedy, M. M. (1979). Generalizing from single case studies. *Evaluation Quarterly, 3*, 661–678.

Kent, R. N., & Foster, S. L. (1979). Direct observational procedures: Methodological issues in naturalistic settings. In A. R. Ciminero, K. S. Calhoun, & H. E. Adams (Eds.), *Handbook of behavioral assessment* (279–324). New York: John Wiley & Sons.

Kiresuk, T. J., & Garwick, G. (1975). Basic goal attainment scaling procedures. In B. R. Compton & B. Galaway (Eds.), *Social work processes* (pp. 388–401). Homewood, IL: The Dorsey Press.

Kiresuk, T. J., & Lund, S. H. (1978). Goal attainment scaling. In C. C. Atkisson, W. A. Hargreave, M. J. Horowitz, & S. E. Sorenson (Eds.), *Evaluation of human service programs* (pp. 341–368). New York: Academic Press.

Kratochwill, T. R. (1978). *Single subject research: Strategies for evaluating change*. New York: Academic Press.

Krippendorff, K. (1980). *Content analysis: An introduction to its methodology*. Beverly Hills, Calif.: Sage Publications.

Lazare, A. (1979). Hypothesis testing in the clinical interview: The psychiatric examination in the walk-in clinic. *Archives of General Psychiatry, 33*, 96–102.

Mager, R. F. (1972). *Goal analysis*. Belmont, CA: Fearon.

Mahoney, M. J. (1978). Experimental methods and outcome evaluation. *Journal of Consulting and Cinical Psychology, 46*(4), 660–672.

Martens, W. M., & Holmstrup, E. (1974). Problem-oriented recording. *Social Casework, 55*, 554–561.

Miller, D. C. (1977). *Handbook of research design and social measurement*. New York: David McKay Co.

Mitchell, J. V. Jr. (Ed.)(1968). *Tests in print III*. Lincoln: University of Nebraska Press.

Mutschler, E. (1979). Using single-case evaluation procedures in a family and children's service agency: Integration of practice and research. *Journal of Social Service Research, 3*, 115–134.

NASW Code of Ethics (rev. ed. 1980). New York: National Association of Social Workers.

Nay, W. (1979). *Multimethod clinical assessment*. New York: Gardner Press.

Nelsen, J. C. (1985). Verifying the independent variable in single-subject research. *Social Work Research and Abstracts, 21*, 3–8.

Neugeboren, B. (1985). *Organization, policy, and practice in the human services*. New York: Longman.

Neuhring, E. M., & Pascone A. B. (1986). Single-subject evaluation: A tool for quality assurance. *Social Work, 31*, 359–365.

Nurius, P. S. (1983). Use of time-series analysis in the evaluation of change due to intervention. *The Journal of Applied Behavioral Science, 19*, 215–228.

Ogilvie, D. M., Stone, P. J., Kelley, E. F., Dixon, B., Bouma, G. B. J., & Atkinson (1987). Computer-aided content analysis. In R. B. Smith & P. K. Manning (Eds.), *Handbook of social science research methods* (pp. 122–141). New York: Oxford University Press.

Parsonson, B. S., & Baer, D. M. (1978). The analysis and presentation of graphic data. In T. R. Kratochwill. (Ed.), *Single subject research: Strategies for evaluating change* (pp. 101–162). New York: Academic Press.

Peters, T. (1987). *Thriving on chaos: Handbook for a management revolution*. New York: Knopf.

Peterson, D. (1968). *Clinical study of social behavior*. New York: Appleton.

Piliavin, I., & McDonald, T. (1978). On the fruits of evaluative research for the social services. In S. Slavin (Ed.), *Social Administration: The Management of the Social Services* (pp. 337–343). New York: Haworth.

Power, G., Meenagham, T. M., & Toomey, B. (1985). *Practice focused research: Integrating human service practice and research*. Englewood Cliffs, NJ: Prentice-Hall.

Randall, R. B. (1972). Errors frequently made in using the problem-oriented system. In J. W. Hurst & H. K. Walter (Eds.), *The problem-oriented system* (pp. 67–71). New York: Medcom.

Reamer, F. (1982). *Ethical dilemmas in social service*. New York: Columbia University Press.

Rinn, R. C., & Vernon, J. C. (1975). Process evaluation of outpatient treatment in a community mental health center. *Journal of Behavior Therapy and Experimental Psychiatry, 6,* 5–11.

Rock, B. D. (1987). Goal and outcome in social work practice. *Social Work, 32,* 393–398.

Rosen, R., & Proctor, E. K. (1978). Specifying the treatment process: The basis for effectiveness research. *Journal of Social Service Research, 2,* 25–43.

Rubin, A. (1985). Practice effectiveness: More grounds for optimism. *Social Work, 30,* 469–476.

Rubin, A. (1986). Tunnel vision in the search for effective intervention: Rubin response. *Social Work, 31,* 403–404.

Russell, B. (1976). *Mysticism and logic.* New York: Barnes & Noble.

Seaberg, J. R., & Gillespie, D. F. (1977). Goal attainment scaling: a critique. *Social Work Research and Abstracts, 13,* 4–9.

Shontz, F., & Rosenak, C. (1985). Models for clinically relevant research. *Professional Psychology: Research & Practice, 16,* 296–300.

Siegel, D. H. (1984). Defining empirically based practice. *Social Work, 29,* 325–329.

Steinem, G. (1983). *Outrageous acts and everyday rebellions.* New York: Holt, Rinehart and Winston.

Strupp, H. H., & Bloxom, A. S. (1975). *Therapists assessment of outcomes: Psychotherapy change measures.* Rockville, MD: National Institute of Mental Health (U.S. Government Printing Office).

Thomas, E. J. (1960). Uses of research methods in interpersonal practice. In N. A. Polansky (Ed.), *Social Work Research* (pp. 254–283). Chicago, IL: University of Chicago Press.

Thompson, J. D. (1967). *Organizations in action.* Chicago, IL: McGraw-Hill.

Timms, N., & Timms, R. (1977). *Perspectives in social work.* London: Routledge & Kegan Paul.

Van de Ven, A., Delbecq, A. L., & Koenig, R. (1976). Determinants of coordination modes within organizations, *American Sociological Review, 41,* 322–338.

Van de Ven, A., & Ferry, D. (1980). *Measuring and assessing organizations.* New York: John Wiley & Sons.

Wallace, W. (1971). *The logic of science in sociology.* New York: Aldine Publishing Company.

Walls, R. T., Werner, T. J., Bacon, A., & Zane, T. (1977). Behavior checklists. In J. D. Cone & R. P. Hawkins (Eds.), *Behavioral assessment* (pp. 77–146). New York: Brunner/Mazel.

Webb, E. J., Campbell, D. T., Schwartz, R. D., & Sechrest, L. (1981). *Unobtrusive measures: Nonreactive research in the social sciences.* Chicago, IL: University of Chicago Press.

Weber, R. P. (1985). *Basic content analysis.* Beverly Hills, Calif.: Sage Publications.

Whiteman, M., Fanshel, D., & Grundy, J. F. (1987). Cognitive-behavioral interventions aimed at anger of parents at risk of child abuse, *Social Work, 32,* 469–474.

Witkin, S. L., & Harrison, D. F. (1979). Single-case designs in marital research and therapy. *Journal of Social Service Research, 3*, 51–66.

Wolf, F. A. (1989). *Taking the quantum leap: The new physics for nonscientists*. New York: Harper & Row.

Wolf, M. M. (1978). Social validity: The case for subjective measurement or how applied behavior analysis is finding its heart. *Journal of Applied Behavior Analysis, 11*, 203–214.

Yin, R. K. (1984). *Case study research: Design and methods*. Beverly Hills, CA: Sage Publications.

Zimbalist, S. E. (1983). The single-case clinical research design in developmental perspective: Mainstream or tangent? *Journal of Education for Social Work, 19*, 61–66.

Appendix A
The Self-Assessment Checklist

To plan a self-assessment of your practice, ask yourself the following questions and design your project based upon the answers.

Is what I want to evaluate best studied by focusing on individual clients/ client systems over time, or on multiple clients at one (or two) times?
√ If the answer is many clients, then choose a large-scale group design.
√ If the answer is an individual client/client system, then choose a single-subject design.

Who do I want to study?
√ If you want to learn something about yourself, then choose yourself. Self-knowledge is a most valuable asset to all social workers—micro and macro practitioners.
√ If you want to learn something about the effect of your work on your clients, then choose a client/client system as the target.

Can I specify the independent variable (the intervention)?
√ If the answer is no, then choose process evaluation. The purpose of this assessment would be to study your intervention process. If you cannot specify with some degree of clarity what you do, you should begin your evaluation program with a process evaluation.
√ If the answer is yes, then choose outcome evaluation. The purpose of this assessment would be to study the effect of what you do. This requires that you specify what you are doing clearly enough so that you can repeat the general format, and so that another person reading your description could closely replicate your technique.

How, then, should I ask the research question?

√ If you want to know how (or how well) you use a technology, ask the research question such that you are studying your use of the technology independent of the specific client system (process evaluation/self as target).

√ If you want to know how (or how well) you use a technology with a particular client/client system, ask the research question such that you are focusing on the interaction of the technology with your client/client system (process evaluation/client as target).

√ If you want to know how the technology is impacting your practice, ask the research question such that you can assess how the technology is affecting you independent of particular clients. In this situation, you must specify the independent variable (outcome evaluation/self as target).

√ If you want to know how the technology is impacting the client/client system, ask the research question such that you are measuring the impact of the technology independent of yourself. In this situation, you must specify the independent variable (outcome evaluation/client as target).

Can I specify the dependent variable (the outcome)?

√ If the answer is no, then choose a qualitative approach. In this situation you cannot be specific about what it is you will measure in order to know whether your intervention was effective. You may, or may not, be able to be specific about the intervention.

- If you do not understand the situation in any way, you must start with a case study design. This will help you describe the problem.
- If you can be fairly specific about the problem but cannot specify the goal in great detail, we recommend the target problem approach.
- If you can be specific about the problem and the goal of the intervention, but not about the intervention itself, the goal attainment approach will work well.

√ If the answer is yes, then choose a quantitative approach. It is important that your measure be a clear indicator of the problem expected to change or the expected outcome of the intervention.

- If you can be specific about both the desired outcome and the intervention, but cannot measure the dependent variable during a baseline period, use the single-subject monitoring design.

- If you can be specific about both the desired outcome and the intervention and can take at least three baseline measurements, then the single-subject quasi-experimental or multiple baseline design is the appropriate design.

Can I operationalize the independent variable (my intervention) and/or the dependent variable (the outcome of my intervention)? With what will I collect/measure the data?
√ Recordings?
√ Logs or journals?
√ Protocols?
√ Survey questionnaire?
√ Behavioral measures?
√ Standardized instruments?

From whom will I collect the data?
√ Multiple observers are often needed in order to have reliable data. Collect it from multiple sources. Just because the target of single-subject research is one individual, this does not negate the possibility of collecting data from two or more sources. Any of the following are appropriate sources of data:

- the client or client system
- outside expert consultants
- peers and colleagues
- yourself

What shall I do with the data?
√ Chapter 5 provides several approaches to analyzing your data. The analysis you choose depends upon the variability of your data and the answers you seek.

What do I do with the information after I have analyzed the data?
√ If you find what you expected, you should integrate this knowledge into your practice, state a new hypothesis in more specific terms, and test it with a new assessment project.
√ If you find something extremely different from what you expected, you should repeat the study to verify this finding and adjust your interventions in accordance with this new data.

SUMMARY CHECKLIST

What is the purpose of
my study?
_____
_____
_____

I therefore choose a . . . group design ___   single system design ___

Who is the target of
my study?   me ___   my client ___

Can you specify the
independent variable
(the intervention)?   yes ___   no ___
I therefore choose a . . . process evaluation ___   outcome evaluation ___

How, then, will I ask the
research question?
_____
_____
_____

Which design, then, will
I choose?   Case study _____   Monitoring _____
                       Target problem _____   Baseline _____
                       GAS _____   Multiple _____

Am I able to
operationalize the   yes ___   no ___
independent variable? how? _____
                       _____

Am I able to
operationalize the   yes ___   no ___
dependent variable?   how? _____

What is my
measurement tool?   _____
Whom am I collecting
data from?   _____

Have I submitted my
design to Human
Subjects Review?   yes ___   no ___

**How will I analyze my
data?**

_____

_____

_____

**How will I disseminate
the results of my study?**

_____

_____

_____

Appendix B
100+ Outcome Variables

MICRO LEVEL

Weight (reduce or increase)
Cigarette smoking (reduce)
Obscene language (reduce use)
Telephone calls (increase positive use)
Sexual behavior (increase satisfaction)

Drugs (reduce dependence)
Procrastination (reduce)
Lateness (reduce or eliminate)
Treatment/therapy (maintain)
Daily management (maintain)

Marital conflict (reduce)
Anger (instances of feeling)
Physical fighting (reduce instances)
Belittling (reduce instances)
Drinking alcohol (reduce consumption)

Moodiness (decrease)
Use of medication (reduce)
Study behavior (best use of time)
Pain (relieve)
Diet (maintain)

Shopping (control spending)
Child–parent interaction (increase)
Ulcer attack (reduce)
Gallstone attack (reduce)
Exercising (increase)

Arguing (reduce instances)
Television watching (reduce hours)
Aggression (reduce instances)
Class attendance (increase)
Reading speed (increase)

Driving in traffic (reduce
  frustration)
Sleeping (reduce/increase hours)
Interpersonal contact (increase)
Study habits (increase output)
Shyness (become more outgoing)

Childhood discipline (reduce
  instances)
Coffee consumption (reduce)
Eye contact (increase)
Fear (reduce)
Accomplishments (increase)

Assertiveness (increase instances)
Use of time (increase positive use)
Ability to give (increase)

Acts of aggression (reduce)
Number of times you say "yes"
  when you really mean "no"
  (reduce)
Anxiety (reduce amount)
Embarrassment (reduce instances)

Calories (maintain desired level)
Dependency on others (reduce)
Feedback to child (increase)
Attention to self (increase time)
Express feeling (increase instances)

Time together (increase)
Relaxation (increase ability)
Worrying (reduce)
Images of self (improve)

MACRO LEVEL

Staff morale (improve)
Supervisory interaction (increase)
Assertiveness (increase)
Employee use of time (improve)
Aggressiveness (decrease)

Attendance (reduce absenteeism)
Procrastination (reduce)
Time management (improve)
Risk-taking behavior (increase)
Stress (reduce)

Employee participation (increase)
Employee effectiveness (increase)
Employee efficiency (increase)
Employee morale (maintain)
Employee enthusiasm (increase)

Hiring successfully (improve skill)
Firing successfully (improve skill)
Handling grievances (improve)
Handling conflict (improve)
Flexibility to changing demands

Team building (improve skill)
Leadership of task groups
  (improve)
Openness to staff (increase)
Openness to board (increase)
Innovating (increase)

Performance evaluation (improve
  skill)
Soliciting support (improve skill)
Capturing resources (improve skill)
Finding opportunities (increase)
Political sensitivity (improve skill)

Own morale (increase)
Influencing others (increase skill)
Ability to delegate (improve)
Ability to say no/yes (improve)
Willingness to risk (improve)

Empowering others (improve skill)
Dependency of others on you
    (decrease)
Dependency of you on others
    (decrease)
Interaction between others
    (increase)
Participation of others (increase)

Planning (increase skill)
Organizing (increase skill)
Budgeting (increase skill)
Accounting (increase skill)
Record maintenance (increase skill)

Coordinating (improve skill)
Negotiating (improve skill)
Arbitrating (improve skill)
Integrating (improve skill)
Confronting (improve skill)

Problem solving (improve skill)
Ethics (improve awareness)
Decision making (improve)
Staff development (increase)
Solicit/use of diversity (increase)

Affirmative action (increase)
Minority recruitment (increase)
Comparable worth (increase)
Allocative justice (increase)
Community sanction (create)

Adapted from Behling & Merves, 1984, pp. 32–33.

Appendix C
Annotated Bibliography of Books of Scales

This is not a comprehensive inventory of psychosocial scales. It is simply a list of references that are readily available and in current use in clinical practice.

Brodsky, S. L., & O'Neal Smitherman, H. (1983). *Handbook of scales for research in crime and delinquency.* New York: Plenum.

This book reviews most established tests in current use in the field of crime and delinquency. It provides samples of the instruments and standardization data, explains scoring procedures, and suggests uses for the instruments. The scales provided cover the broad range of research in crime and delinquency.

Corcoran, K., & Fischer, J. (1987). *Measures for clinical practice: A sourcebook.* New York: Free Press.

This book is specifically designed to provide social work practitioners with instruments to help them evaluate their practices. It reviews several scales covering a broad range of clinical interests. Scoring procedures, reliability, validity, and recommended areas of applicability are provided. Of particular usefulness are tables at the front of the book that reference scales by population and by content area. This feature makes referencing a particular scale for a particular use easy and fast.

Hudson, W. W. (1982). *The Clinical Measurement Package: A field manual.* Chicago: Dorsey.

Hudson provides nine scales covering a wide range of clinical problems. The scales may be used as a package or as individual scales. He provides all of the reliability and validity data for the scales and information as to reliability and validity with specific populations. The scoring is standardized and cut points are established, making these scales easy to use and score.

Mitchell, J. V., Jr. (Ed.) (1983). *Tests in print III.* Lincoln: University of Nebraska.

This book provides a listing of nearly every test that is available commercially. For each scale it provides a brief summary and references to reliability and validity studies. It identifies the target population for each instrument and provides information about uses that have been reported. It indexes tests by name, target population, and content area.

Appendix D
Microcomputer Software
for Self-Assessments

The software market is constantly changing, so we will not describe specific software packages in detail. Any such descriptions would be outdated within months. Rather, we have listed the major types of software that are useful for completing self-assessment projects. The software listed below is available in almost overwhelming variety for any type of hardware.

Although we will list the software types separately, in many cases they are available in integrated packages: that is, two or more types of software are combined and available in one package. For example, much of Chapter 4 was produced using Microsoft Excel©, an integrated package consisting of database, spreadsheet, and statistical and graphics functions. It is very convenient to use integrated packages because you do not have to open and close each type of software as you use it, but can move between functions without loss of time.

The software packages you will need for self-assessment projects are as follows:

WORD PROCESSING

For preparing any kind of text, word processing programs save enormous amounts of time. This is because, unlike most typewriters, when you strike a key the letter/image appears on the screen, but not on the paper. You can therefore edit—change letters, move sentences and paragraphs, delete, add, and format—swiftly and without having to retype the entire document

each time you must make changes or produce another draft. You can make
"hard copies" (copy printed on paper) when you are completely done.

For example, many people no longer use pencil and paper for writing.
Caseworkers and therapists (with good typing skills) have reported that by
writing case notes, keeping logs and journals, and doing reports on their
desktop computers, the quantity and quality of their work has improved
greatly.

Further, and as noted in Chapter 5, there are some analytic purposes
to which word processing programs can be put. Most good packages have
"global search" functions that allow you to find within the text any specific
word or phrase you wish. This function can be used for doing content analysis of transcripts, case notes, process recordings, newspapers, or any other
source of data in text form that is in your computer.

SPREADSHEETS

This is just what the name implies, an electronic piece of graph paper. You
can set up tables by typing titles and column headings, and then enter
numbers (or text) in rows and columns. As with word processing, you can
play around with the table on the screen—adding, deleting, changing—
until it is formatted to your liking. Then you make a hard copy if you want.

Spreadsheet applications are created by entering formulas wherever
you want the program to do a calculation or compute a statistic. All spreadsheets do basic mathematical calculations (add, subtract, multiply, and divide). Many spreadsheets will also compute statistics (mean, mode, max,
min, variance, square root, standard deviation, correlation), as well as
trend, logarithmic, and trigonometric functions.

For example, you could set up a spreadsheet to compute effect size
(ES) and then routinely enter the data you obtain from single-subject monitoring or experimental projects. You would thereafter, without pain and
effort, have a record of your intervention outcome and an index of client
change. You can also set up spreadsheets to test for autocorrelation and to
remove serial dependency by means of transformations. Appendixes F and
G demonstrate the use of spreadsheets in these ways.

GRAPHICS

Graphic packages vary greatly, from those created for use by artists to
those with more limited capabilities. For the purposes of self-assessment
projects, a modest business graphics package is all that is needed.

For example, the line charts and scattergrams in Chapter 4 were produced using computer graphics. All we did was enter the data into a spreadsheet and command the computer to produce the chart. In fact, we could have chosen bar, pie, or box charts or histograms. For most single-subject data, however, the line chart is the most descriptive.

STATISTICAL PACKAGES

If you do not have access to a multifunction spreadsheet with statistical capability, you can purchase a statistical package for a modest sum (under $50). Many of the newer statistical packages allow you to enter data into a spreadsheet (rather than "on line"—(using a terminal to enter data on a mainframe computer) a holdover from the mainframe packages) and will calculate all of the statistics you will ever need in social work practice. Unless you are doing survey research with tens of thousands of cases requiring multivariate analytic procedures, these new statistical packages will more than meet your requirements. They are simple to use and generally have good documentation.

Appendix E
Human Subjects Review

All research involving human subjects done within an institution by faculty or students requires human subjects review. Such research done by social workers in private practice or within private organizations should be held to the same standards concerning the protection and rights of human subjects.

Some social work research qualifies for *exempt status*, meaning that the risk to subjects is minimal and that the subjects' rights of informed consent and confidentiality are assured by the research design. If a research project meets the requirements for exempt status, it does not have to be reviewed by the institution's Human Subjects Committee. There is usually a person designated within each institutional department or unit to review research projects *before* they are implemented for the purpose of granting exempt status. If exempt status is not granted, then the project is more than minimal risk and the design must be reviewed by the institution's Human Subjects Review Committee.

The questions listed below are a means of establishing whether your research meets the standard of minimal risk. A negative response to any item means that your research does not put your subjects at minimal risk or that their rights are not ensured and, therefore, your research must be reviewed by the Human Subjects Review Committee (if you are a student or faculty member), or that you should consult a research specialist if outside an institution.

MINIMAL RISK

The following questions pertain to the level or risk involved in your research project. Please answer each question with either a "yes" or a "no."

_____Will the participant experience any pain or physical danger?

_____Will the participant experience any emotional arousal or psychological stress (such as anxiety, discomfort, or frustration) beyond the levels normally expected in everyday life?

_____Will the project induce or attempt to induce long-term, significant change in the participant's behavior (including attitudes toward self and others)?

_____Will the data embarrass or socially disadvantage the participant were confidentiality to be violated?*

_____Will there be any concealment or misinformation such that the participant might choose not to participate in the research had (s)he been aware of the true state of affairs?

_____Will the project respect the participant's cultural, religious, or personal values?

COMPONENTS OF CONSENT

Informed consent refers to a competent person's freely given decision to participate in a research project based on full knowledge of relevant aspects of the project and the implications of participation for the participant's welfare. Place an X before each statement that the investigator plans on following.

I will provide the participant:

_____A fair explanation of the procedures to be followed, including reference to any use of data-gathering techniques entailing audio- or videotape, still or motion picture, or any other means of capturing and storing information about the participant.

_____A description of any attendant discomforts or risks.

_____An offer to answer any questions about the procedures.

_____An instruction that the participant is free to decline participation and is free to withdraw consent and discontinue participation at any time without any loss of benefits or other negative consequences.

*Please note that a project is more than minimal risk if the information would embarrass the subject were confidentiality to be violated. Thus, survey research involving sensitive material is not exempt, even when confidentiality is maintained, because it is more than minimal risk.

CONFIDENTIALITY

All data collected from participants must be kept confidential. Information about a participant should not be associated with identifying characteristics of the individual (e.g., name, photograph, or unique status attributes) in the report on the results of the project or in any material made available to individuals not conducting the research.

Confidentiality is assured by: (check one)
　　　____Anonymous responses
　　　____A coding system that is in a secured location that is separate from
　　　the responses
　　　____Other (explain) _____

Appendix F
Creating Templates for Statistical Tests

Included in this appendix are printouts of four templates that can be copied to create your own spreadsheets for doing the statistical computations described in Chapter 5. They are:

1. Test for Autocorrelation
2. Removing serial dependency by means of First Differences Transformation
3. Removing serial dependency by means of Moving Averages Transformation
4. Effect Size (ES)

Although they look formidable to someone not acquainted with microcomputer spreadsheets, these were not difficult to create. We used Microsoft Excel© (a commercial program), entered the formula for each step in row 2, and "copied" it down the rest of the column. For anyone with some spreadsheet experience, the time needed for creating these templates is minimal—no more than an hour.

When you have created a spreadsheet with these formulas, all you need to do is enter your raw scores in column A (we allowed space for 29 scores, but you could create many more rows if necessary). Once the scores are entered (it takes about a minute), the spreadsheet will calculate the statistic in a second. Most integrated packages such as Excel© will also allow you to generate a scatterplot and line chart directly from the spreadsheet. This can save you hours of work if you have been doing it manually.

Appendix G contains printouts of spreadsheets showing the formulas for the tests and transformations described in Chapter 3. It also includes illustrations of what the spreadsheet would look like if you entered data as we have done with the following example.

A social work educator who taught Research Methods in an M.S.W. program decided she needed to stimulate her students to become more interested in research. If they weren't truly motivated to learn these methods, she thought, they certainly would not use them once they were in practice. One way of motivating students was to write case examples that illustrated the use of difficult designs in different settings. These she would use as handouts in class and, with carefully crafted discussion questions, would see if she could overcome their resistance to applied research and engender enthusiasm for trying self-assessment designs in their practica. She decided that one indicator of teaching effectiveness would be to count the minutes that students sustained discussion and questions when the handouts were introduced into the class. She asked a teaching assistant to time the discussions. She introduced the case examples during the fifth class, and these were the results:

FIGURE F.1.   Time-series data showing number of minutes spent in discussion each of 14 days.

Class	Discussion (minutes)	Class	Discussion (minutes)
1	10	8	32
2	17	9	40
3	16	10	45
4	14	11	35
5	20	12	48
6	30	13	50
7	26	14	55

It is obvious from eyeballing these data that there is an intervention effect. The following spreadsheet templates were used to tell us more.

1. *Autocorrelation*. Is this data autocorrelated? To find out, we entered the data shown in Figure F.1 into the Autocorrelation Template shown in Apendix G-1. The illustration in Appendix G-2 shows that the data were indeed autocorrelated; the correlation is $r = .63$, which is well above the index of $r = .53$.
2. *First Differences Transformation*. Can this serial dependency be removed? The data in Figure F.1 were entered into the First Dif-

ferences Template shown in Appendix G-3. The results in Appendix G-4 show that this transformation did not remove the serial dependency; correlation is $r = .74$, which is well above the index of $r = .55$.

3. *Moving Averages Transformation*. The data in Figure F.1 were entered into the Moving Averages Template shown in Appendix G-5. The results illustrated in Appendix G-6 show that the autocorrelation is $r = .54$, while the index is $r = .85$. The Moving Averages technique did remove the dependency.

4. *Effect Size (ES)*. To obtain an index of intervention effect, use the absolute values (ignore the signs) of the transformed data from the First Differences illustration (column B in Appendix G-4) and enter them into columns A and B in the Effect Size Template as shown in Appendix G-7. The results are shown in Appendix G-8. The change ceated by the social work teacher is assessed by comparing the four baseline class periods with the intervention class periods. The index of change was 3.44 (found in cell C31), which is standardized by dividing by the standard deviation of the change score, producing an Effect Size of 1.15 (found in cell F31). When multiplied by K, the corrected ES is 1.03 (found in cell F33). Consulting a Table of the Normal Curve (a z-table), the interpretation of this finding is that discussion time improved by 35% over the average discussion time before the intervention. To this teacher, this is probably a successful outcome, even though the corrected ES would have to reach 1.96 for conventional statistical significance.

Appendix G
Templates for Time Series Analysis

G-1 Autocorrelation Template

	A	B	C	D	E
1	Score (S)	(S - Mean)	Moving Products	(X-Mean)sqrt	Bartlett's Test
2		=IF(A2="","",(A2-A32))		=IF(B2="","",(B2*B2))	Autocorrelation
3		=IF(A3="","",(A3-A32))	=IF(B3="","",(B3*B2))	=IF(B3="","",(B3*B3))	r =
4		=IF(A4="","",(A4-A32))	=IF(B4="","",(B4*B3))	=IF(B4="","",(B4*B4))	=(C31/D31)
5		=IF(A5="","",(A5-A32))	=IF(B5="","",(B5*B4))	=IF(B5="","",(B5*B5))	
6		=IF(A6="","",(A6-A32))	=IF(B6="","",(B6*B5))	=IF(B6="","",(B6*B6))	
7		=IF(A7="","",(A7-A32))	=IF(B7="","",(B7*B6))	=IF(B7="","",(B7*B7))	is r > than
8		=IF(A8="","",(A8-A32))	=IF(B8="","",(B8*B7))	=IF(B8="","",(B8*B8))	2/sqrt (n)?
9		=IF(A9="","",(A9-A32))	=IF(B9="","",(B9*B8))	=IF(B9="","",(B9*B9))	=(2/A34)
10		=IF(A10="","",(A10-A32))	=IF(B10="","",(B10*B9))	=IF(B10="","",(B10*B10))	
11		=IF(A11="","",(A11-A32))	=IF(B11="","",(B11*B10))	=IF(B11="","",(B11*B11))	If YES, then the
12		=IF(A12="","",(A12-A32))	=IF(B12="","",(B12*B11))	=IF(B12="","",(B12*B12))	data are
13		=IF(A13="","",(A13-A32))	=IF(B13="","",(B13*B12))	=IF(B13="","",(B13*B13))	Autocorrelated
14		=IF(A14="","",(A14-A32))	=IF(B14="","",(B14*B13))	=IF(B14="","",(B14*B14))	
15		=IF(A15="","",(A15-A32))	=IF(B15="","",(B15*B14))	=IF(B15="","",(B15*B15))	
16		=IF(A16="","",(A16-A32))	=IF(B16="","",(B16*B15))	=IF(B16="","",(B16*B16))	
17		=IF(A17="","",(A17-A32))	=IF(B17="","",(B17*B16))	=IF(B17="","",(B17*B17))	
18		=IF(A18="","",(A18-A32))	=IF(B18="","",(B18*B17))	=IF(B18="","",(B18*B18))	
19		=IF(A19="","",(A19-A32))	=IF(B19="","",(B19*B18))	=IF(B19="","",(B19*B19))	
20		=IF(A20="","",(A20-A32))	=IF(B20="","",(B20*B19))	=IF(B20="","",(B20*B20))	
21		=IF(A21="","",(A21-A32))	=IF(B21="","",(B21*B20))	=IF(B21="","",(B21*B21))	
22		=IF(A22="","",(A22-A32))	=IF(B22="","",(B22*B21))	=IF(B22="","",(B22*B22))	
23		=IF(A23="","",(A23-A32))	=IF(B23="","",(B23*B22))	=IF(B23="","",(B23*B23))	
24		=IF(A24="","",(A24-A32))	=IF(B24="","",(B24*B23))	=IF(B24="","",(B24*B24))	
25		=IF(A25="","",(A25-A32))	=IF(B25="","",(B25*B24))	=IF(B25="","",(B25*B25))	
26		=IF(A26="","",(A26-A32))	=IF(B26="","",(B26*B25))	=IF(B26="","",(B26*B26))	
27		=IF(A27="","",(A27-A32))	=IF(B27="","",(B27*B26))	=IF(B27="","",(B27*B27))	
28		=IF(A28="","",(A28-A32))	=IF(B28="","",(B28*B27))	=IF(B28="","",(B28*B28))	
29		=IF(A29="","",(A29-A32))	=IF(B29="","",(B29*B28))	=IF(B29="","",(B29*B29))	
30		=IF(A30="","",(A30-A32))	=IF(B30="","",(B30*B29))	=IF(B30="","",(B30*B30))	
31	=SUM(A2:A30)		=SUM(C2:C30)	=SUM(D2:D30)	
32	=AVERAGE(A2:A30)				
33	=COUNT(A2:A30)				
34	=SQRT(A33)				

G-2 Autocorrelation Illustration

	A	B	C	D	E
1	Score (S)	(S - Mean)	Moving Products	(S-Mean)sqrt	Bartlett's Test
2	10	-5.2	16.36	26.69	
3	12	-3.2	19.53	10.03	Autocorrelation
4	9	-6.2	7.19	38.03	r =
5	14	-1.2	2.53	1.36	.63
6	13	-2.2	6.86	4.69	
7	12	-3.2	-2.64	10.03	is r > than
8	16	0.8	4.03	0.69	2/sqrt (n)?
9	20	4.8	23.36	23.36	.58
10	20	4.8	13.69	23.36	
11	18	2.8	8.03	8.03	If YES, then the
12	18	2.8	13.69	8.03	data are
13	20	4.8		23.36	Autocorrelated
14					
15					
16					
17					
18					
19					
20					
21					
22					
23					
24					
25					
26					
27					
28					
29					
30					
31	182		112.64	177.67	
32	15.17				
33	12				
34	3.46				

G-3 First Differences Transformation Template

	A	B	C	D	E	F
1	Score (S)	difference	(S - Mean)	Moving Products	(S-Mean)sqrt	Bartlett's Test
2		=IF(A3<1,"",(A3-A2))	=IF(B2="","",(B2-B32))	=IF(C3="","",(C3*C2))	=IF(C2="","",(C2*C2))	
3		=IF(A4<1,"",(A4-A3))	=IF(B3="","",(B3-B32))	=IF(C4="","",(C4*C3))	=IF(C3="","",(C3*C3))	
4		=IF(A5<1,"",(A5-A4))	=IF(B4="","",(B4-B32))	=IF(C5="","",(C5*C4))	=IF(C4="","",(C4*C4))	Autocorrelation
5		=IF(A6<1,"",(A6-A5))	=IF(B5="","",(B5-B32))	=IF(C6="","",(C6*C5))	=IF(C5="","",(C5*C5))	r=
6		=IF(A7<1,"",(A7-A6))	=IF(B6="","",(B6-B32))	=IF(C7="","",(C7*C6))	=IF(C6="","",(C6*C6))	=(D31/E31)
7		=IF(A8<1,"",(A8-A7))	=IF(B7="","",(B7-B32))	=IF(C8="","",(C8*C7))	=IF(C7="","",(C7*C7))	(ignore the sign)
8		=IF(A9<1,"",(A9-A8))	=IF(B8="","",(B8-B32))	=IF(C9="","",(C9*C8))	=IF(C8="","",(C8*C8))	
9		=IF(A10<1,"",(A10-A9))	=IF(B9="","",(B9-B32))	=IF(C10="","",(C10*C9))	=IF(C9="","",(C9*C9))	is r > than
10		=IF(A11<1,"",(A11-A10))	=IF(B10="","",(B10-B32))	=IF(C11="","",(C11*C10))	=IF(C10="","",(C10*C10))	2/sqrt (n)?=
11		=IF(A12<1,"",(A12-A11))	=IF(B11="","",(B11-B32))	=IF(C12="","",(C12*C11))	=IF(C11="","",(C11*C11))	=(2/B34)
12		=IF(A13<1,"",(A13-A12))	=IF(B12="","",(B12-B32))	=IF(C13="","",(C13*C12))	=IF(C12="","",(C12*C12))	
13		=IF(A14<1,"",(A14-A13))	=IF(B13="","",(B13-B32))	=IF(C14="","",(C14*C13))	=IF(C13="","",(C13*C13))	If YES, then the
14		=IF(A15<1,"",(A15-A14))	=IF(B14="","",(B14-B32))	=IF(C15="","",(C15*C14))	=IF(C14="","",(C14*C14))	data are still
15		=IF(A16<1,"",(A16-A15))	=IF(B15="","",(B15-B32))	=IF(C16="","",(C16*C15))	=IF(C15="","",(C15*C15))	Autocorrelated
16		=IF(A17<1,"",(A17-A16))	=IF(B16="","",(B16-B32))	=IF(C17="","",(C17*C16))	=IF(C16="","",(C16*C16))	
17		=IF(A18<1,"",(A18-A17))	=IF(B17="","",(B17-B32))	=IF(C18="","",(C18*C17))	=IF(C17="","",(C17*C17))	If NO, then the
18		=IF(A19<1,"",(A19-A18))	=IF(B18="","",(B18-B32))	=IF(C19="","",(C19*C18))	=IF(C18="","",(C18*C18))	serial dependency
19		=IF(A20<1,"",(A20-A19))	=IF(B19="","",(B19-B32))	=IF(C20="","",(C20*C19))	=IF(C19="","",(C19*C19))	has been removed
20		=IF(A21<1,"",(A21-A20))	=IF(B20="","",(B20-B32))	=IF(C21="","",(C21*C20))	=IF(C20="","",(C20*C20))	
21		=IF(A22<1,"",(A22-A21))	=IF(B21="","",(B21-B32))	=IF(C22="","",(C22*C21))	=IF(C21="","",(C21*C21))	
22		=IF(A23<1,"",(A23-A22))	=IF(B22="","",(B22-B32))	=IF(C23="","",(C23*C22))	=IF(C22="","",(C22*C22))	
23		=IF(A24<1,"",(A24-A23))	=IF(B23="","",(B23-B32))	=IF(C24="","",(C24*C23))	=IF(C23="","",(C23*C23))	
24		=IF(A25<1,"",(A25-A24))	=IF(B24="","",(B24-B32))	=IF(C25="","",(C25*C24))	=IF(C24="","",(C24*C24))	
25		=IF(A26<1,"",(A26-A25))	=IF(B25="","",(B25-B32))	=IF(C26="","",(C26*C25))	=IF(C25="","",(C25*C25))	
26		=IF(A27<1,"",(A27-A26))	=IF(B26="","",(B26-B32))	=IF(C27="","",(C27*C26))	=IF(C26="","",(C26*C26))	
27		=IF(A28<1,"",(A28-A27))	=IF(B27="","",(B27-B32))	=IF(C28="","",(C28*C27))	=IF(C27="","",(C27*C27))	
28		=IF(A29<1,"",(A29-A28))	=IF(B28="","",(B28-B32))	=IF(C29="","",(C29*C28))	=IF(C28="","",(C28*C28))	
29		=IF(A30<1,"",(A30-A29))	=IF(B29="","",(B29-B32))	=IF(C30="","",(C30*C29))	=IF(C29="","",(C29*C29))	
30		=IF(A31<1,"",(A31-A30))	=IF(B30="","",(B30-B32))		=IF(C30="","",(C30*C30))	
31		=SUM(B2:B30)		=SUM(D2:D30)	=SUM(E2:E30)	
32		=AVERAGE(B2:B30)				
33		=COUNT(B2:B30)				
34		=SQRT(B33)				

G-4 First Differences Transformation Illustration

	A	B	C	D	E	F
1	Score (S)	difference	(S - Mean)	Moving Products	(S-Mean)sqrt	Bartlett's Test
2		2.0	1.4	-2.24	1.92	
3		-1.0	-1.6	-2.24	2.61	
4		2.0	1.4	-0.85	1.92	Autocorrelation
5		0.0	-0.6	-0.24	0.38	r=
6		1.0	0.4	0.15	0.15	-.74
7		1.0	0.4	0.15	0.15	(ignore the sign)
8		1.0	0.4	-1.01	0.15	
9		-2.0	-2.6	-6.24	6.84	is r > than
10		3.0	2.4	-3.85	5.69	2/sqrt (n)?=
11		-1.0	-1.6	-0.62	2.61	.55
12		1.0	0.4	0.15	0.15	
13		1.0	0.4	-0.24	0.15	If YES, then the
14		0.0	-0.6		0.38	data are still
15						Autocorrelated
16						
17						If NO, then the
18						serial dependency
19						has been removed
20						
21						
22						
23						
24						
25						
26						
27						
28						
29						
30						
31		8		-17.07	23.08	
32		0.62				
33		13				
34		3.61				

G-5 Moving Averages Transformation Template

	A	B	C	D	E	F
1	Score (S)	Moving Average	(S - Mean)	Moving Products	(S-Mean)sqrt	Bartlett's Test
2		=IF(A3<1,"",AVERAGE(A2:A3))	=IF(B2="","",(B2-B33))	=IF(C4="","",(C4*C2))	=IF(C2="","",(C2*C2))	
3						
4		=IF(A5<1,"",AVERAGE(A4:A5))	=IF(B4="","",(B4-B33))	=IF(C6="","",(C6*C4))	=IF(C4="","",(C4*C4))	Autocorrelation
5						
6		=IF(A7<1,"",AVERAGE(A6:A7))	=IF(B6="","",(B6-B33))	=IF(C8="","",(C8*C6))	=IF(C6="","",(C6*C6))	r=
7						=(D31/E31)
8		=IF(A9<1,"",AVERAGE(A8:A9))	=IF(B8="","",(B8-B33))	=IF(C10="","",(C10*C8))	=IF(C8="","",(C8*C8))	(ignore the sign)
9						
10		=IF(A11<1,"",AVERAGE(A10:A11))	=IF(B10="","",(B10-B33))	=IF(C12="","",(C12*C10))	=IF(C10="","",(C10*C10))	is r > than
11						2/sqrt (n)?=
12		=IF(A13<1,"",AVERAGE(A12:A13))	=IF(B12="","",(B12-B33))	=IF(C14="","",(C14*C12))	=IF(C12="","",(C12*C12))	=(2/B34)
13						If YES, then the
14		=IF(A15<1,"",AVERAGE(A14:A15))	=IF(B14="","",(B14-B33))	=IF(C16="","",(C16*C14))	=IF(C14="","",(C14*C14))	data are still
15						Autocorrelated
16		=IF(A17<1,"",AVERAGE(A16:A17))	=IF(B16="","",(B16-B33))	=IF(C18="","",(C18*C16))	=IF(C16="","",(C16*C16))	
17						
18		=IF(A19<1,"",AVERAGE(A18:A19))	=IF(B18="","",(B18-B33))	=IF(C20="","",(C20+D20+D18*C18)	=IF(C18="","",(C18*C18))	If NO, then the
19						serial dependency
20		=IF(A21<1,"",AVERAGE(A20:A21))	=IF(B20="","",(B20-B33))	=IF(C22="","",(C22*C20))	=IF(C20="","",(C20*C20))	has been removed
21						
22		=IF(A23<1,"",AVERAGE(A22:A23))	=IF(B22="","",(B22-B33))	=IF(C24="","",(C24*C22))	=IF(C22="","",(C22*C22))	
23						
24		=IF(A25<1,"",AVERAGE(A24:A25))	=IF(B24="","",(B24-B33))	=IF(C26="","",(C26*C24))	=IF(C24="","",(C24*C24))	
25						
26		=IF(A27<1,"",AVERAGE(A26:A27))	=IF(B26="","",(B26-B33))	=IF(C28="","",(C28*C26))	=IF(C26="","",(C26*C26))	
27						
28		=IF(A29<1,"",AVERAGE(A28:A29))	=IF(B28="","",(B28-B33))	=IF(C30="","",(C30*C28))	=IF(C28="","",(C28*C28))	
29						
30		=IF(A31<1,"",AVERAGE(A30:A31))		=SUM(D2:D30)	=SUM(E2:E30)	
31		=SUM(B2:B30)				
32		=COUNT(B2:B30)				
33		=(B31/B32)				
34		=SQRT(B33)				

184

G-6 Moving Averages Transformation Illustration

	A	B	C	D	E	F
1	Score (S)	Moving Average	(S - Mean)	Moving Products	(S-Mean)sqrt	Bartlett's Test
2		2.0	-3.6	9.18	12.76	
3						
4		3.0	-2.6	2.76	6.61	Autocorrelation
5						r=
6		4.5	-1.1	-0.99	1.15	.54
7						(ignore the sign)
8		6.5	0.9	0.86	0.86	
9						is r > than
10		6.5	0.9	1.79	0.86	2/sqrt (n)?=
11						.85
12		7.5	1.9	6.61	3.72	
13						If YES, then the
14		9.0	3.4		11.76	data are still
15						Autocorrelated
16						
17						If NO, then the
18						serial dependency
19						has been removed
20						
21						
22						
23						
24						
25						
26						
27						
28						
29						
30						
31		39		20.21	37.71	
32		7				
33		5.57				
34		2.36				

G-7 Effect Size Template (Including Hedge's Correction)

	A	B	C	D	E	F
1	Baseline	Intervention	Change Scores		Table:Hedge's	Correction factor
2		Scores (B)	(B-A)		N-1	K
3	7	10	=IF(B3="","",(B3-A32))		2	0.56419
4	1	4	=IF(B4="","",(B4-A32))		3	0.7236
5	2	6	=IF(B5="","",(B5-A32))		4	0.79788
6	6	8	=IF(B6="","",(B6-A32))		5	0.84075
7		5	=IF(B7="","",(B7-A32))		6	0.86863
8		10	=IF(B8="","",(B8-A32))		7	0.8882
9		13	=IF(B9="","",(B9-A32))		8	0.9027
10		2	=IF(B10="","",(B10-A32))		9	0.91387
11		5	=IF(B11="","",(B11-A32))		10	0.92275
12			=IF(B12="","",(B12-A32))		11	0.92996
13			=IF(B13="","",(B13-A32))		12	0.93594
14			=IF(B14="","",(B14-A32))		13	0.94098
15			=IF(B15="","",(B15-A32))		14	0.94529
16			=IF(B16="","",(B16-A32))		15	0.94901
17			=IF(B17="","",(B17-A32))		16	0.95225
18			=IF(B18="","",(B18-A32))		17	0.95511
19			=IF(B19="","",(B19-A32))		18	0.95765
20			=IF(B20="","",(B20-A32))		19	0.95991
21			=IF(B21="","",(B21-A32))			
22			=IF(B22="","",(B22-A32))			
23			=IF(B23="","",(B23-A32))			
24			=IF(B24="","",(B24-A32))			
25			=IF(B25="","",(B25-A32))			
26			=IF(B26="","",(B26-A32))			
27			=IF(B27="","",(B27-A32))			
28			=IF(B28="","",(B28-A32))			
29			=IF(B29="","",(B29-A32))			
30			=IF(B30="","",(B30-A32))			
31	=SUM(A3:A30)		=AVERAGE(C3:C30)		EFFECT SIZE=	=(C31/C32)
32	=AVERAGE(A3:A30		=STDEV(C3:C30)		CORRECTION K:=VLOOKUP(B34,E2:F20,2)	
33	=COUNT(A3:A30)	=COUNT(B3:B30)			CORRECTED ES=(F31*F32)	
34	=(A33-1)	=(B33-1)				

G-8 Effect Size Illustration

	A	B	C	D	E	F
1	Baseline	Intervention	Change Scores		Table:Hedge's	Correction factor
2	Scores (A)	Scores (B)	(B-A)		N-1	K
3	7	10	6		2	.56419
4	1	4	0		3	.72360
5	2	6	2		4	.79788
6	6	8	4		5	.84075
7		5	1		6	.86863
8		10	6		7	.88820
9		13	9		8	.90270
10		2	2		9	.91387
11		5	1		10	.92275
12					11	.92996
13					12	.93594
14					13	.94098
15					14	.94529
16					15	.94901
17					16	.95225
18					17	.95511
19					18	.95765
20					19	.95991
21						
22						
23						
24						
25						
26						
27						
28						
29						
30						
31	16		3.44		EFFECT SIZE=	1.15
32	4		3.00		CORRECTION K=	.90270
33	4	9			CORRECTED ES=	1.03
34	3	8				
35						

Index